"Lance is doing some of the most importan
ing for people's souls. In *High-Impact Teams*, ne takes it to another level,
showing you how health can meet high performance. Here's the great news
Lance shares: you don't need to sacrifice performance to get healthy, nor
do you need to sacrifice health to perform."

Carey Nieuwhof, founding pastor, Connexus Church

"During my many years of working with churches, I've seen spiritually and
emotionally healthy teams accomplish very little because no real attention
was paid to performance. I've also seen high-performing teams experience
brief moments of accomplishment only to fall apart because the team
wasn't healthy. Finally, we have a book that helps us tackle both health
and performance. It's only through the 'and' that churches can develop
truly high-impact teams."

Tony Morgan, lead strategist and founder, The Unstuck Group

"You are holding the best book you can ever read with your team. With
Lance as an expert guide, learn to go faster and further as you grow healthier
together."

Will Mancini, founder, Auxano; author, *God Dreams*

"Lance lives and breathes team. *High-Impact Teams* is a great resource for
helping you build a healthy and high-performing team."

John Ortberg, senior pastor, Menlo Church; author, *I'd
Like You More If You Were More Like Me*

"If you are building a team or are on a team, get this book. It's the absolute
best single resource I've ever come across. This book is a gold mine for team
development and problem-solving, delivered in short, bite-size chapters.
The chapter titled 'Doing vs. Developing' alone is worth the price of the
book. I am deeply indebted to Lance's teaching and coaching of me and
our staff the last few years. As we have applied the principles in this book,
the results have been so encouraging—health and productivity."

Chip Ingram, teaching pastor, Living on the Edge; author, *The Real God*

"Lance Witt is a master at building healthy and effective teams—and this book is more evidence that we can all learn from his expertise and wisdom. Read this book, but don't do it alone. As your entire team processes this book together, you will grow in synergy, partnership, and achievement."

Lee Strobel, bestselling author and professor
at Houston Baptist University

"Lance Witt is a pastor's pastor and knows firsthand the challenges of leading with both courage and compassion. He combines personal experience with keen insight into Scripture to provide practical guidelines. *High-Impact Teams* is the perfect field guide for anyone who wants to strengthen their team and their relationship with God."

Chris Hodges, senior pastor, Church of the Highlands;
author, *Fresh Air* and *The Daniel Dilemma*

"Lance Witt proves he understands the power of teamwork and the importance of personal health in *High-Impact Teams*. It's challenging, hope-filled, and full of practical ideas that will increase your leadership capacity and strengthen your teams. This book should be shared and read often."

Doug Fields, author, speaker, consultant

"For four years now, Lance Witt has been my coach. We meet together, Skype, email, and talk on the phone. His insight, experience, and wisdom have drastically improved my leadership. But he is only one guy and his calendar fills up. That is why this incredible book is such a gift. Welcome to Lance's unique classroom; you will be a more caring and effective leader if you pull up a chair."

Pete Briscoe, senior pastor, Bent Tree Bible Fellowship

"Lance Witt consistently reminds me that 'healthy things grow.' Lance is one of the best go-to resources for pastoral health in the world. Now he brings his knowledge to the team level. No matter what size your church or team is, you can be healthier. Which means you can grow more. Start now by reading *High-Impact Teams*."

William Vanderbloemen, CEO and founder, Vanderbloemen Search Group

"Through powerful and inspirational stories, Lance Witt compellingly unpacks the importance of building healthy and effective teams. The principles found in this book are based on Scripture, but that doesn't mean it's for only pastors. This book is a must-read for *all* leaders. If you read this book with an open heart and mind, I know you'll receive revelation and insight to strengthen your leadership skills and build teams that perform at the highest levels."

Robert Morris, founding senior pastor, Gateway Church; bestselling author, *The Blessed Life*, *The God I Never Knew*, and *Frequency*

"Healthy teams are essential to healthy churches. In *High-Impact Teams*, Lance Witt clearly defines what a healthy, high-impact team is really made of—and gives us all the game plan for building many of them. Lance's wisdom and insight come from years in the trenches doing the hard work of good team building. I'm beyond excited to have this resource to study with my staff and volunteer team leaders at The Journey."

Nelson Searcy, founder and lead pastor, The Journey Church NYC; founder, Church Leader Insights, www .churchleaderinsights.com; author, *The Renegade Pastor*

"Lance has a heart for God, a passion for people, and a healthy approach to ministry that he practices and preaches. He is a seasoned ministry veteran who has not let the waves of ministry capsize him. Marinate in the wisdom of this book and you will find health in the midst of high impact. Having this book is like having a coach with you at all times."

Craig Jutila, family pastor, Venture Christian Church; founder and president, Empowered Living; author, *Hectic to Healthy*

"We all want to be part of a healthy team. In this biblically based, easy-to-read book, Lance provides the key principles and tools needed to move your team toward greater health and productivity. I will be calling on all our staff teams to go through it together and highly recommend you do the same. On this topic, I am not aware of a more valuable resource and will be referring to it for years to come."

Dr. Henry Schorr, Centre Street Church, Calgary, Alberta, Canada

"My friend Lance Witt is unusually gifted in discerning the needs of leaders and extraordinarily clear in communicating strategies for health and fruitful ministry impact. Through his speaking, consulting, and writing, Lance has brought countless leaders from the brink of burnout to the strike zone of spiritual fruitfulness. This book delivers Lance's wisdom right to the heart of the staff meeting, the board room, and the very culture of your organization. As you absorb the principles of *High-Impact Teams*, you will become a better leader, your organization will embrace better rhythms, and the people you serve will be deeply grateful."

Daniel Henderson, president, Strategic Renewal
International; author, *Old Paths, New Power*

HIGH-IMPACT TEAMS

HIGH-IMPACT TEAMS

WHERE HEALTHY MEETS HIGH PERFORMANCE

LANCE WITT

BakerBooks

a division of Baker Publishing Group
Grand Rapids, Michigan

© 2018 by Lance Witt

Published by Baker Books
a division of Baker Publishing Group
PO Box 6287, Grand Rapids, MI 49516-6287
www.bakerbooks.com

Printed in the United States of America

Library of Congress Cataloging-in-Publication Data
Names: Witt, Lance, author.
Title: High-impact teams : where healthy meets high performance / Lance Witt.
Description: Grand Rapids : Baker Publishing Group, 2018. | Includes bibliographical
    references.
Identifiers: LCCN 2018007038 | ISBN 9780801075681 (pbk.)
Subjects: LCSH: Church group work. | Christian leadership.
Classification: LCC BV652.2 .W58 2018 | DDC 253/.7—dc23
LC record available at https://lccn.loc.gov/2018007038

18   19   20   21   22   23   24   7   6   5   4   3   2   1

Whatever I am and whatever God chooses to do through me is because of the relationships I have had. And through the years many of those relationships have been team members. I am forever indebted to the teams I have served with in ministry. You have sharpened me, loved me, stretched me, forgiven me, prayed for me, believed in me, and supported me. It has been a great ride, and I am filled with gratitude.

Contents

Contents

Yorker is suing his parents for "indifference to his problems." And a high school student from Somerdale, New Jersey, was kicked off the track team for multiple unexcused absences. His father filed a $40 million lawsuit claiming the dismissal will cost his son college scholarships.

When it comes to your life, you hold the position of CLO: chief life officer. That doesn't mean you control everything in your world, but it does mean you are responsible for leading yourself.

I remember a season when I was not living well. I was an executive pastor at Saddleback Church with Rick Warren. It was a rapid-change, fast-paced, high-demand kind of environment. Add to that my own tendencies toward workaholism and people pleasing and you had the perfect recipe for an unhealthy soul.

Everyone in my family was doing the best they could to make life work during those crazy days. But occasionally the stress would become too much, and my wife, Connie, and I would have one of those "come to Jesus" conversations. Connie is one of the most unpretentious people you will ever meet, and you never have to wonder what she's thinking. She's a lousy hypocrite. In fact, our family sometimes kiddingly says she's never had a private thought in her life. In those moments of tense conversation, she would say, "You're never home. The kids don't get the time they need with you, and I sure don't get any quality time with you. And even when you're home, you're not really home. You're always on the phone or on email."

At that point I would skillfully try to lay down my "victim card." I would say, "It's just for a season." Translation: "I am a victim of my circumstances. When we get through Easter it will be better." Or "When we get through this campaign, things are going to slow down."

In moments of sheer frustration, Connie would interrupt me as I was playing my victim card and say, "Just stop it. It never changes. There is always another season, some new opportunity or problem that keeps you from being with us."

In one of our more heated discussions, she took off the gloves and with more than a little hurt and frustration said, "There is always a reason or a season why you can't be who you are supposed to be." Her words stung. But she was absolutely right.

I was not a victim. No one was holding a gun to my head. I was making choices about how I was living, and many of those choices were poor ones. I had to face the reality that I was who I was because of choices I had made.

One of the best days of my life was the day I began to take personal responsibility for the health of my own soul and life.

Here is the good news. The life you long for, the life your soul craves, is accessible. And it has nothing to do with your job description, the size of your church or organization, or your place on the org chart. The abundant life Jesus talks about in John 10 can actually be your real-life experience. According to 2 Peter 1:3, "By his divine power, God has given us everything we need for living a godly life" (NLT). Everything!

Deuteronomy 30 contains a fascinating passage that illustrates this truth. The first ten verses show that God extended an invitation to a blessed life. The Lord said that when the Israelites decided to return and follow Him with a whole heart, He would give them an abundant and rich life. He promised to restore their fortunes, increase their number, and protect them from their enemies. Then, in verse 9, we read, "The LORD your God will then make you successful in everything you do. He will give you many children and numerous livestock, and he will cause your fields to produce abundant harvests, for the LORD will again delight in being good to you as he was to your ancestors" (NLT).

It is an incredible passage of hope and promise. Right on the heels of this offer of a blessed life, God took away the possibility of the Israelites playing the victim card. He said, "Now what I am commanding you today is not too difficult for you or beyond your reach. It is not up in heaven, so that you have to ask, 'Who will ascend into heaven to get it and proclaim it to us so we may obey it?' Nor is it beyond the sea, so that you have to ask, 'Who will cross the sea to get it and proclaim it to us so we may obey it?' No, the word is very near you; it is in your mouth and in your heart so you may obey it" (Deut. 30:11–14).

This abundant, rich, satisfying, fulfilling, meaningful, joy-filled life is accessible. In the words of Deuteronomy 30, it is not too difficult, and it is not out of reach. It is close at hand and available.

A few verses later in Deuteronomy 30:19, the Lord said, "Today I have given you the choice between life and death, between blessings and curses.

Now I call on heaven and earth to witness the choice you make. Oh, that you would choose life, so that you and your descendants might live!" (NLT).

God says He has given us the choice between life and death, blessings and curses. Choosing life seems like a no-brainer. But how many times have we chosen ways that are destructive and hurtful instead of life-giving? I want us to be very clear about one thing from this passage: the life of blessing is a choice.

Then, with a sense of pleading, God said, "Oh, that you would choose life." Let those words seep down into your soul.

And if the Israelites would "choose life," they and their descendants would live. I don't think God was talking about the length of their lives as much as He was talking about the quality of their lives. Leading yourself well and caring for yourself is not selfish; it is good stewardship. And you will not only have a richer life personally but also bring your best self to your team.

The starting point in building a great team is to "choose life." Take personal responsibility. Own it. Put your victim card in the trash and start leading yourself well.

TEAM DISCUSSION QUESTIONS

1. Either in your personal life or ministry, when are you most apt to play the victim card?

2. Read Deuteronomy 30:11–14 again. What word or phrase most stands out to you? Why?

3. God says the abundant life is not out of reach or too difficult. It really can be ours. What would an abundant, rich, and meaningful team experience look like?

4. What is one area where you could better lead yourself?

PART 2

BRING YOUR
BEST YOU

Any discussion about teams has to start with individuals, because great teams are made up of healthy and high-performing individuals. This book is written on the foundational premise that the greatest gift you give your team is a healthy and high-performing you. In this section, we will explore issues of personal and emotional health and how they impact team health.

Doing Ministry
without Losing Your Soul

I have been a Christ-follower for more than forty-five years and in ministry for more than forty years. Even as I stare at those words, it is hard to believe. My mind races back to a weekend retreat in Glorieta, New Mexico, where I had the first inkling of a desire for life in ministry. I was a seventh grader, and it was my first ever student retreat. One night after the evening session, we were divided into groups to pray together. I was put with a couple of high school seniors and a friend they had brought who didn't attend our church. I remember the four of us sitting around the base of a tree at about 10:30 at night. It was a perfect fall evening, with a bright moon. I was both intimidated and excited to be grouped with these high school kids. Before we prayed, the two high school seniors from my youth group began to share the gospel with their friend. The Holy Spirit had obviously prepared his heart, because he immediately embraced the idea of becoming a follower of Jesus. Right there, that tree became his altar and he gave his life to Christ.

I can still remember that moonlit night and how it felt to see somebody's life changed by the power of the gospel. I didn't really have much of a concept of ministry at that point, but I remember thinking, *I would love to help other people experience the power of Christ's love.*

As a fairly new Christ-follower, my love for Christ was pure, naïve, simple, passionate, and wholehearted. About five years later, I sensed a call from God to give my life to ministry. I certainly didn't fully understand all that I was signing up for, but I couldn't imagine giving my life to anything more important. And for more than forty years I have tried to live out that call.

Like any other relationship, my walk with Jesus the last four decades has had a lot of ups and downs. Those words that described my adolescent love for Jesus haven't always reflected my relationship with Christ through the years. My love hasn't always been pure; I have at times been driven by motives that were more about me than Jesus. My love for Christ certainly isn't naïve anymore. Little surprises or shocks me. Forty-plus years of ministry down in the trenches will shatter your rose-colored glasses.

I don't know that I would call my love for Christ simple these days. Ministry complicates your love for Jesus. My love for Jesus now has a ministry job attached to it. It was years before I realized that loving ministry and loving Jesus are not necessarily the same. As far as my love for Christ being passionate and wholehearted, I have certainly experienced seasons when those words accurately described my love for Christ. But the truth is, in other seasons my spiritual life has been stale, stuck, and disconnected. I have also had seasons when my loyalty and love have been divided. Sometimes my people pleasing, absence of courage, ambition to succeed, lack of faith, insecurities, and compulsive busyness have chipped away at my wholehearted devotion.

Nothing is more internally conflicting than trying to inspire people to be passionate about God when you have little or no passion yourself. Nothing is more hollow than trying to connect people to God when you feel disconnected from Him. To me, it's like going to church when you and your spouse aren't speaking. You put up the façade and pretend everything is okay while you're there, but you walk away knowing that everything isn't. What you portrayed publicly isn't what you're experiencing privately.

At this point in life I have a more realistic, seasoned-by-life view of loving Jesus. If you have been in ministry more than a week, you know that serving Jesus isn't always filled with Kumbaya moments, Holy Ghost goose bumps, or prayers of salvation on a moonlit night.

I can relate to Henri Nouwen's words as he writes of his own spiritual struggles after years of ministry:

> I began to experience a deep inner threat. As I entered my fifties and was able to realize the unlikelihood of doubling my years, I came face to face with the simple question, 'Did becoming older bring me closer to Jesus?' After twenty-five years of priesthood, I found myself praying poorly, living somewhat isolated from other people, and very much pre-occupied with burning issues. Everyone was saying that I was doing really well, but something inside was telling me that my success was putting my own soul in danger.[1]

While the specific symptoms of spiritual drift might be different for each of us, Nouwen's question is worth pondering. As you get older and serve in ministry longer, are you getting closer to Jesus? That is a sobering and convicting question for me to reflect on.

The truth is, for much of my ministry this issue wasn't really on my radar. I was preoccupied with growing my church, impacting our community, managing the budget, preparing my sermons, and developing as a leader. Biblically I certainly knew that loving and knowing Jesus were to be my highest priorities. But if you examined how I spent my time, what I thought about, what I read, what motivated me, and what I talked about, it would have been obvious that a deep and loving relationship with Jesus was down on the list. An honest audit of my life would have revealed that my deepest longings were about ministry success.

I can relate to Kyle Strobel's honest confession in the book *The Way of the Dragon or the Way of the Lamb*: "I had healthy intentions to be faithful and grow in Christ. But my desire for power was stronger than those intentions and my desire came to the surface quickly."[2]

What the authors call power, I would refer to as unhealthy ambition.

They go on to say that "our feet are trained to find paths of self-achievement and self-glorification. We use our vocations to build significance. We use our relationships to get ahead."[3]

The older I get, the more painfully aware I become that my ambition has a shadow side. A healthy ambition, marked by humility and governed by the Holy Spirit, is an amazing quality. But when it gets hijacked by my ego or need to be seen as a success, it becomes toxic for my soul.

This reality highlights the tensions we live with in ministry. Doing vs. being. Caring for others vs. caring for self. Waiting on God vs. working for God. Praying vs. planning. Preparing spiritual meals for others vs. feeding ourselves. Measurable deliverables vs. the unmeasurable work of the Spirit. Depth vs. breadth. God working in us vs. God working through us. In ministry, we must hold these tensions carefully. None of the tensions listed are either/or propositions. They are both/and. In fact, embracing only one side of the tension leads to either distorted thinking or dysfunction.

The gravitational pull in the twenty-first century is toward doing, leading, driving, and growing. None of those are negative unless they cause us to neglect having a healthy soul that is deeply pursuing a vibrant relationship with Jesus. A life focused only on the doing/achieving side of the tension will lead to distorted motives, a skewed view of success, and dysfunction on the team.

As Ruth Haley Barton writes, "It is possible to gain the world of ministry success and lose your own soul in the midst of it all."[4]

I have experienced seasons when I was so preoccupied with building the ministry and helping everyone else live the Christian life that I neglected my own spiritual life. We must intentionally pursue a loving relationship with Jesus as a beloved son or daughter, not as a professional minister. We must also pursue Christ in community with our team. In the healthiest team cultures, we take time for spiritual conversations, we challenge and encourage spiritual growth, we open God's Word together, we speak about what God is doing in our lives, and we regularly stop to pray with one another.

Deuteronomy 30, the passage I referred to in the last chapter, concludes with an important challenge. In the first part of that final verse, the people are implored to "love the LORD your God, listen to his voice, and hold fast to him" (v. 20). The key to experiencing this amazing life God offers is to be intentional about pursuing your relationship with Him.

That, my friend, is your highest calling. Your deep and growing relationship with Jesus is one of the greatest gifts you will ever give your teammates. But the passage doesn't end there. The next six words are the pinnacle of the entire chapter: "For the LORD is your life."

Let those words wash over you for a moment. He doesn't say, "Your ministry is your life." Nor does he say, "Your church or nonprofit is your life." He doesn't even say, "Your family is your life." You see, someday your ministry position is going to go away. Someone else is going to take over your nonprofit. Someone else will move into your office and throw your business cards in the trash. No matter how "successful" you have been, someday the spotlight will shift to someone else. But if you have been pursuing Jesus and He is your life, it will be okay. Because your relationship with Him transcends your role, your position, your title, your platform, and your ministry.

For the Lord is your *life*.

TEAM DISCUSSION QUESTIONS

1. What three words would you use to describe your spiritual life these days?
2. How would you honestly assess your pursuit of Jesus over the last year?
3. What do you think would raise your team's spiritual vitality?
4. How could your team encourage and support you in your pursuit to love Jesus?

The Greatest Gift You Give Your Team

I have lived most of my life (even as a pastor) with a cognitive knowledge that I had a soul, but almost no awareness that I was supposed to pay attention to it. Biblically I knew God had saved my soul, but experientially in my day-to-day life, I hardly gave my soul (inner life) a second thought.

That misdirected living has had significant consequences and touched every one of my relationships (including those with members of my team) and every part of my life. When you don't pay attention to your soul, you naturally end up putting all your focus on the externals of your life. You feed and fuel the doing side of your life while starving the being side.

When Parker Palmer talks about the journey of the soul, he remarks, "Everything in us cries out against it—which is why we externalize everything. It is so much easier to deal with the external world, to spend our lives manipulating material and institutions and other people instead of dealing with our own soul."[1]

By the way, that's a great recipe for the making of a Pharisee.

My natural wiring is to be ambitious and driven, and in some ways those qualities have served me well. But what I didn't comprehend is that there was a shadow side to those traits. Often my ambition, which I saw as a strength, was motivated not by God's glory but by an unhealthy need to be perceived as a success. Over time I learned how to cloak my selfish ambition in kingdom language. It became easy to wrap my unhealthy ambition in God talk and sanctify it. This ultimately led to some unhealthy behavior and thinking: posturing in conversations, name dropping, number fudging, obsessing over leadership and growth, and ultimately a utilitarian view of people.

A cousin to my unhealthy ambition was my drivenness. This led to being compulsively busy and always trying to live beyond my limits. I believed the lie that important people are busy people. I often wore my busyness as a badge of honor. And I had no trouble rationalizing my insane pace, because after all, I was doing it for Jesus.

I was also completely oblivious to scripts that I had been carrying since my childhood. One of those scripts that I have now been able to identify was to "make sure everybody has a good opinion of you." This, of course, led to an unhealthy people pleasing and approval addiction.

These are all issues of the soul and emotional health, and they also impacted the teams I worked with. My drivenness manifested itself in impatience with results, defensiveness, criticizing, applauding workaholism, and putting projects over people. I'm sure the people I served with could expand on that list.

I am finally beginning to learn that people who are emotional adolescents will never be great team leaders.

A friend of mine was in a team meeting where palpable conflict was present in the room. As he described the leader's reaction, he likened him to "the fifth-grade bully on the elementary playground." Through defensiveness and intimidation, the leader quickly shut down the conflict and the conversation. Everyone in the room "turtled up." And I guarantee you it will be a long time before they venture out of their shells again. The leader's lack of emotional health and self-awareness had a devastating impact on their team health.

Pete Scazzero is spot-on when he writes, "Emotional health and spiritual maturity are inseparable."[2]

When I became a Christ-follower, almost all my discipleship was about the externals. In fact, I would describe my church's attempt to disciple me as mostly "behavior modification." Stop saying certain words. Start reading your Bible. Stop going certain places. Start volunteering in the church. Stop chasing materialism. Start tithing.

And while there was an external (doing) part of my discipleship, what was never really talked about was the transformation that needed to happen in my inner life (being). We never discussed emotions or what might be driving my life under the surface of my actions.

We all know people who have been saved for forty years and are biblically knowledgeable. They have sat through thousands of sermons, and they faithfully attend everything at the church. They have held leadership positions, and they tithe faithfully. But their emotional disposition doesn't match someone who has been hanging around Jesus and His people for forty years. Instead of increasing in love and compassion, they are crotchety, critical, and mean. A glaring disconnect exists between their outward actions and their emotional health. They are broken emotionally, and everybody sees it but them.

Honestly, confronting your emotional health is one of the hardest things you will ever do.

The apostle Paul highlights the importance of your inner life in 2 Corinthians 7:1: "Therefore, since we have these promises, dear friends, let us purify ourselves from everything that contaminates body and spirit, perfecting holiness out of reverence for God."

It is not just your body that is in danger of being poisoned. Paul says your spirit (inner life) can also be contaminated.

I want to share with you a lesson I wish I had learned much earlier in my life about some toxins that had contaminated my soul. Some of the qualities people applaud in your life are the very things that can wreck your soul. Rewind. Read that last sentence again. Let it soak in and serve as a red-flag warning.

Being productive is great—and I was always patted on the back for my strong work ethic—until it turns into drivenness and workaholism. Then it becomes toxic. Ambition is wonderful when it is motivated by God's glory and governed by the Holy Spirit. But when it gets hijacked by our ego, it is lethal and leaves devastation in its wake. Having good people skills is a wonderful quality for those of us who work in ministry—until we begin to live for the approval of others and find our significance in what they think of us.

The result can be that we end up wearing our dysfunction as a badge of honor. For example, I secretly loved it when people would talk about how hard I worked. But what other people didn't know was there was a shadow side to what they perceived as a strength. I consistently pushed beyond the boundaries of a healthy work ethic. I worked all the time and had no recreational interests, no sense of healthy rhythm, no acknowledgment of my limits, and an out-of-control pace. My soul and my family paid the highest price.

Great Strength	Shadow Side
Commitment to excellence	Obsessive perfectionism
Speaking gifts	Unhealthy need for the spotlight
Attention to detail	High control
Visionary leadership	Use people in the name of vision
Servant-hearted	Codependent and approval addiction
Gets along with everyone	Avoids conflict

When you don't pay attention to your soul, you will try to manage your brokenness by adjusting and rearranging the externals in your life. I always tried to deal with my drivenness by tweaking my schedule. I thought if I could just figure out how to work smarter, I could satisfy my compulsive need to be productive and also live out my stated values and priorities. But it never seemed to work. I always felt compulsively busy and as though I were cheating my family.

One day the Holy Spirit took the spotlight off my calendar and put it on my soul. He began to ask, "So, Lance, why are you so driven? Why are you always compulsively busy? Why can you never say no? What's behind that? Let's talk about that." That moment started me on a path of understanding that began with the realization that my drivenness wasn't a calendar issue; it was an emotional health issue and a shadow issue of the soul.

Pete Scazzero writes, "Your shadow is the accumulation of untamed emotions, less-than-pure motives and thoughts that, while largely unconscious, strongly influence and shape your behaviors. It is the damaged but mostly hidden version of who you are."[3]

The darkest part of your shadow side is found lurking around your gifting. What makes this so insidious is that we learn from an early age to mask our lack of emotional health. Others usually see it earlier and more clearly than we do.

When I am walking down the street on a sunny day, I rarely notice my shadow. It is subtle, but it is real. The same is true with my emotional shadow side. If you are going to move toward emotional health, you must be intentional to grow in self-awareness. As I heard it said recently, self-awareness is the only defense against self-deceit. Spending time in solitude, practicing the discipline of self-reflection, reading books about the ways of the soul, and seeking honest input from friends are all crucial to becoming more self-aware.

The French author François Fénelon writes, "We have an amazing ability to self-deceive. Your self-interest hides in a million clever disguises."[4]

That is so true. I have spent a lot of time reflecting on this issue of self-awareness. And I have come up with a list of things that can keep you blinded to the issues of emotional health:

- Minimize the importance of the soul and the inner life.
- Stiff-arm people who try to speak into your life.
- Ignore your own emotions and feelings.
- Don't consider how your lifelong scripts have shaped you.
- Don't explore how your past (family of origin and experiences) has impacted your present.
- Don't have any space in your calendar or your life. Constant busyness keeps you from being reflective and having the space to be with and hear God. As Pete Scazzero says of busy leaders, "They do more activity for God than their relationship with God can sustain."[5]
- Give more priority to everybody's spiritual life (sanctification) than to your own.
- Find your worth and significance in your accomplishments and achievements (doing) rather than in your relationship with God and your identity as His child (being).

- Fail to acknowledge your shadow side and its dangers. "By failing to look at our shadows, we feed a dangerous delusion that leaders too often indulge: that our efforts are always well intended, our power is always benign, and the problem is always in those difficult people whom we are trying to lead!"[6]

Facing your shadow side is not only about self-awareness; it is also about courage. Facing your shadow side and addressing emotional health is not only disruptive and uncomfortable for you but also unsettling for those around you.

Let me explain. Let's suppose you are the person on the team who has always been the available, accessible, get-it-done, go-to individual. You have established a kind of social contract with your team. When people need something, they often call you, and you drop whatever you are doing to respond to their need. Part of your motivation is driven by an authentic desire to serve. But then you begin to realize that some of your response is driven by codependency tendencies as well as a need to please others. The situation has become unhealthy, and it is taking a toll on you and your family. You decide that you need to implement some healthy boundaries to protect your own soul and the health of your family. You are going to start employing the word *no*. You are going to turn off your phone at night so you can be present with your family. You just changed the social contract . . . and trust me, not everyone is going to be thrilled.

Let me give you another quick example. Let's suppose you are the person on the team who has an engaging, warm, winsome, likable personality. You are a bit of a pied piper, and people love being around you. However, the honest truth is that you have always skated by on your personality. And it has created some dysfunction. Your shadow side is a lack of diligence and a tendency toward laziness. And as you become more self-aware and seek honest feedback, you discover that your shadow side has done some damage to the team. While people truly like you, they resent that you don't seem to be a hard worker. And they begrudge feeling like they have to cover for you sometimes.

Pursuing emotional health is certainly more art than science. There is no three-step formula for achieving emotional health. It is a slow, gradual, incremental, and daily process. Most days I can't feel any real progress. But if I look back a decade, I am overwhelmed with gratitude for the good work God has done in me. Most days I like the person I am today better than the person I was a decade ago. And while I am far from being the poster child for emotional health, I can honestly say my soul is at rest.

I believe the greatest gift you will give your team is your own healthy soul. I also believe the healthiest people on your team hold in tandem their brokenness and blessedness. They are not in denial about their shadow side, and they live with an acute awareness that they are still very much a work in progress. But there is no frantic striving, because they live in the settled reality that they are unconditionally loved and accepted. In fact, living with an awareness of their brokenness makes their blessedness that much sweeter and richer.

TEAM DISCUSSION QUESTIONS

1. Why can't emotional adolescents be great team leaders?

2. As you think about your gifts, what is one shadow side to your gifting?

3. Second Corinthians 7:1 says, "Therefore, since we have these promises, dear friends, let us purify ourselves from everything that contaminates body and spirit, perfecting holiness out of reverence for God." What does emotional health have to do with perfecting holiness?

4. Is it easier for you to embrace your brokenness or your blessedness? Explain.

I Hate the Word *Balance*

You have probably never heard the name Erich Brenn. But in February 1969, he appeared on *The Ed Sullivan Show*. He was so popular that he would appear seven more times on the show. His claim to fame was "plate spinning."

Brenn's routine consisted of spinning five glass bowls on sticks that were four feet long. While spinning the bowls, he would also start spinning eight dinner plates. The idea was to keep everything spinning without letting a plate or bowl crash to the ground. Just as a bowl would begin to wobble and look as if it would drop, Brenn would frantically run over and get it spinning again. It was both intriguing and stressful to watch.

That sounds like the average week in the life of ministry, doesn't it?

Plate spinning has become a metaphor for how many of us live our lives. We frantically move through our week trying to keep all of the plates in our ministry life and personal life from dropping. It can be exhilarating and exhausting at the same time.

In the past, when I would hear someone talk about living a life of "balance," plate spinning is the picture that came to my mind. I pictured living life in such a way that all my plates were spinning smoothly and nothing was crashing to the floor.

A life of balance has always seemed like a pipe dream, something that just wasn't realistic or attainable. To be honest, I don't think I've ever had a moment of balance in my entire life. I can't think of a single time when every plate in my life and ministry was "spinning" smoothly and effortlessly.

Life is messy and ministry is demanding. On top of that reality, we live in a world poisoned by sin and we have an adversary who roams around like a roaring lion seeking to bring our plates crashing down.

As you can probably tell, I hate the word *balance*. But I love the word *rhythm*. Rhythm portrays something very different. Balance is an illusive dream, but rhythm is a beautiful dance. Rhythm is a choice I make. It allows for busy seasons and the unexpected. A God-ordained rhythm will allow us to live and lead from a healthy soul.

That rhythm is:

Work ➤ Rest

Produce ➤ Restore

Go hard ➤ Stop

Exert energy ➤ Replenish energy

Empty our bucket ➤ Fill our bucket

Noah BenShea writes, "It's the space between the notes that makes the music."[1] The same is true of life. We must have space (rhythm) between the notes of busyness and ministry to make life work as God designed it.

Yet we live in a world that is unfriendly to a healthy rhythm of life. The speed of life and ministry continues to accelerate. We have 24/7 access to most everything. Therefore, we have more options and opportunities coming our way and less time to make decisions about them.

Did you know that 57 percent of workers have vacation time left at the end of the year? I suspect it might be even higher for people in ministry. And 40 percent of workers say they don't feel like they can justify taking the time off.[2]

You would think that a guy with a ministry called Replenish would have this issue tamed in his life. I wish that were the case. For as long as I can remember, I've been a hurrier. Sometimes I will be walking down the street with my wife and I look around and she is three steps behind me. In a rather frustrated voice she will say to me, "Are you going to walk with me or in front of me?" What I want to say is, "If you hurry up, I'll walk with you." But forty years of marriage has taught me some restraint. Now I just apologize and try to slow down. But whether I am waiting in a line at the airport, listening to a long and drawn-out story, or sitting at a stoplight, I find myself muttering those often repeated five words that are a sign of my battle with rhythm: "Could you please hurry up?"

The truth is, I don't just have a hurried step; I have a hurried spirit. Hurry is more about what's going on inside me than what's going on around me. I hurry not so much because of the external demand but because of the internal drive. As I heard John Ortberg say once, "Hurry is not about a disordered schedule, it is about a disordered heart."

Gradually, I have been learning that speed and intimacy do not make good partners. I can't have a deep relationship with my wife in a hurry. What is true in my marriage is also true in my relationship with God.

This issue of hurry has huge implications for the health of your soul, the vitality of your walk with God, and your interaction with your team. You cannot live life at warp speed without warping your soul.

When you run fast and hard and long, eventually you will drain your soul. You won't really notice it for a while, but you will wake up one day and be emotionally empty and spiritually dry. Ministry will feel hard and frustrating. Team members will get on your nerves more than usual. That is not a fun place to be, especially when the demands of ministry never take a break.

Running on empty will eventually lead to cynicism, disillusionment, and burnout. You are not the exception.

Hardwired into the Universe

We live in a universe defined by rhythm. As you read this sentence you are breathing in rhythm. The average person inhales and exhales fifteen to sixteen times per minute. Your heart beats with a very predictable rhythm. When you get an EKG done, it is to measure the electrical rhythm of your heart. The tide comes in and goes out with a sense of rhythm. Much of the beauty of music is tied to rhythm. Farmers have a rhythm of planting and growing and harvesting.

In Leviticus 25, God gives the command that even the land is to be given a Sabbath every seven years. Even the physical dirt needs a break. Nothing is made to constantly produce. Everything God ever created needs rest and restoration. And you, my friend, are not exempt from that law of the universe.

If you violate this principle of rhythm long enough, you will pay a price. When you ignore a healthy rhythm of life, you end up doing violence to your body, your soul, your relationships, your emotions, and your relationship with God.

I remember getting a call from a hard-driving leader in his early sixties. He had been pushing hard and living beyond his limits for more than thirty years and now he had hit the wall.

Something snapped inside of him and in his words, "My body wouldn't behave anymore."

As we talked about a possible coaching relationship, I will never forget what he said: "Lance, I'm not asking you to help me get back to where I was. I can't ever live like that again; I won't survive. I have to establish a new normal."

While his case is extreme, a lot of us in ministry are on the same trajectory. And his story illustrates what can happen when we embrace a lifestyle that ignores the principle of rhythm.

A Deliberate Choice

As you well know, there is always more that can be done and needs to be done. The needs of your ministry will always outpace your capacity. But you can choose a rhythm that declares even though more is still left to do, you can stop to rest and restore.

Jesus regularly took time to live in the spaces between the notes. He often withdrew from the demands of life to be alone and to be with His Father, even in the midst of overwhelming ministry needs.

Mark 1 narrates how Jesus was in Capernaum and had an incredibly busy day of ministry. He was the guest preacher in the synagogue that morning. During the service He was confronted by demons. I don't know about you, but that feels very intense and draining. Not only did He preach and deal with demons, but He also healed people. After church that day, Jesus went to Peter's house for lunch. While there He healed Peter's mother-in-law. And before He wrapped up his day of ministry, the Bible says the townspeople brought everybody in town who was sick and demon-possessed to Jesus's door. Before He put His head on the pillow, He healed more people and cast out more demons. That is a full day of ministry.

According to Mark 1:35, "Very early in the morning, while it was still dark, Jesus got up, left the house."

If you read only the first part of the verse, you might think to your-self, *Well, He is the Son of God. He probably should get up earlier than everyone else. And He only has three years to launch this revolutionary movement called Christianity. He is probably heading off to another full day of preaching and healing.*

But the last part of verse 35 says He goes off to a solitary place, where he prays. He deliberately chose a rhythm that allowed for space and quiet and time to be with His Father. Interestingly, when the disciples finally found Him, they said to Him, "There is more ministry to do back in the village."

But Jesus responded by telling them they were not going back there, but they were going to new places to preach the gospel. What is implicitly clear in the passage is that Jesus got His next set of instructions from the Father in that place of solitude. I wonder if sometimes the reason we have such difficulty discerning the voice of God is because so much noise and busyness fills our lives. You see, just like in the life of Jesus, space and slow are friends to your spiritual health.

And unlike you, Jesus lived at a time in history when slow was built into the fabric of daily life. The lack of technology and transportation forced people to live life a lot slower. The absence of cars, planes, email, and smartphones made life less frenetic. You and I live in a very different world; therefore, we must be even more intentional about living a life of rhythm that allows for space and rest.

A Gift from God

Too often in my life and ministry, I have tried to live as though I had no limits. Can I remind you and me today that we are *not* named Superpastor or Superminister? God made us humans before He made us ministry leaders, and we have the same limitations as the people we shepherd. We have limited time, energy, capacity, and emotional reserves. God gave us those limits as a gift to remind us that we need a rhythm that allows us to stop and rest and replenish and restore. He also gave us those limits to regularly remind us of our dependence on Him.

The load of ministry will always exceed our limits. If we let the load of ministry determine our pace, we will end up emotionally and spiritually unhealthy. But if we let our limits inform our pace, we can find a healthy, life-giving rhythm.

Because you have limits, that means it's okay not to always be accessible. When you have a tendency toward people pleasing like I do, this can be a huge challenge. When you choose to live within your limits, you will end up disappointing some people. But don't let the expectations of others rob you of a healthy rhythm.

Being Present

Several years ago a very good friend of mine was diagnosed with colon cancer. He went through surgery and extensive treatment and was away from his church role for several months. After he returned to his ministry, he and I grabbed lunch together. I was anxious to ask him a question that I had been wanting to ask him for weeks. I said, "You have just faced a very serious health crisis. You have been away from ministry for a few months and you have had lots of time to reflect and listen to God. What is the most significant thing you have learned in your time away?" Without any hesitation, he responded, "A hurried life damages relationships."

A hurried life will do damage to the relationships you have with your team. I encourage you to slow down—not just metaphorically but physically. Walk slower down the hallway.

And when you are in a conversation with a teammate, give them the gift of your unhurried presence. Look them in the eye. Put your phone down. When you are fully present in conversations and meetings, you're communicating to those on your team that they are valuable.

Stop chasing the illusion of balance and deliberately choose the God-ordained life of rhythm.

How is the pace of your life? Is your schedule overcommitted? Are you living a healthy rhythm? Ask a couple of trusted friends or team members to honestly assess how you are doing with this area of your life.

Let me leave you with a question to ponder. What would it take for *you* personally to have a healthy rhythm of life?

TEAM DISCUSSION QUESTIONS

1. As you think about the pace of your life, where would you place yourself on the line below?

    1_____10

    Unhealthy Rhythm   Healthy Rhythm

2. How would you describe the pace of your life over the last six months?

3. In what ways have you seen an unhealthy rhythm take a toll on you personally and on your team?

4. How would you describe your team's rhythm? And what could you do as a team to ensure a healthy rhythm of ministry life?

Just Stop It

"D ad, I know she's the one." I will never forget that special conversation. It was the day my son Jonathan let me know that he wanted to get engaged to Ryanne. Their very first date had been playing golf together, so he decided that he would propose to her on the eighteenth hole of that same golf course. He and his friend Josh devised a creative plan. First, they took a golf ball, cut it in half, and hollowed it out. Then they placed her engagement ring inside the golf ball and put it back together. On the outside of the golf ball, with a black marker, Jonathan wrote what would be her future initials: RW.

Josh's job was to hide in the trees near the eighteenth green to drop the ball in the hole and video the proposal. But it's sort of hard for Josh to hide anywhere since he is 6′10″. As Ryanne and Jonathan got to the eighteenth hole, when Ryanne wasn't looking, Josh ran onto the green and dropped the special golf ball into the hole.

When they reached the green, Jonathan lagged back so that Ryanne would have to go over to the hole and pull the flag. When she went to pull the flag, she noticed a golf ball lying in the hole. She picked it up, and seeing the initials on the ball said, "Look, it's Rick Warren's golf ball."

Jonathan took the golf ball, got down on one knee, took out the engagement ring, and asked her to marry him. Here's why I tell you that story. Inside that random golf ball was a gift that would forever change Ryanne's life. And inside what I always saw as a random Old Testament teaching is a gift that has forever changed my life.

In the last chapter, I talked about the importance of a healthy rhythm of life. Well, I have good news for you. God has actually given us a practical strategy to help us live a life of rhythm. And that strategy is called Sabbath.

I'm not sure what your church or theological background is, but I grew up in a time and in a church where Sabbath was a nonissue. I knew it was one of the Ten Commandments, but I just assumed it was one of those Old Testament things we didn't do anymore.

For the first thirty years of my Christian life, the concept of Sabbath wasn't even a blip on my spiritual radar. I never heard a sermon or read an article about Sabbath. I lumped Sabbath into the same biblical category as the Bible's prohibition against wearing any garment woven together with two kinds of material or eating shrimp.

I didn't personally know one person who practiced Sabbath. And my philosophy of ministry would have had no room for it. I have a "calling," and that calling demands sacrifice. Life is short; the needs are urgent. I have to squeeze all I can out of every second of every minute. I'll rest when I get to heaven.

When that's your mind-set, there is no room for a theology of rest. All my life, I've been taught how to go and go faster; no one ever taught me how to stop.

In recent years, as I have been on a journey to live from a healthy soul, I have spent a lot of time studying what the Bible says about Sabbath and rhythm.

The concept of Sabbath traces its roots all the way back to creation. After God completed the work of creating the universe, He rested on the seventh day. He moved from creation to reflection. He certainly didn't rest because He was worn out from six straight days of creating. He rested to model for us this principle of rhythm.

This seventh day, the day of rest, was so important that God blessed it and declared it holy.

Remember to observe the Sabbath day by keeping it holy. You have six days each week for your ordinary work, but the seventh day is a Sabbath day of rest dedicated to the LORD your God. (Exod. 20:8–10 NLT)

Notice that God does put value on work. Six days are for working hard and being productive. In fact, I believe that unless you work hard you can't really appreciate the gift of Sabbath. Part of God's design for Sabbath is that it would renew and replenish you. Unless you are expending energy and draining your bucket through hard work the other six days, you can't really appreciate the value of God's replenishing you through the practice of Sabbath.

God loves it when we work hard and unplug hard. Did you know that God loves both Jet Skis and scuba diving? I don't have a Bible verse to back up that statement, but I am sure it is true. Flying across the surface of the water at forty miles an hour is fun and exhilarating. You can go fast and cover a lot of territory in a short time. There is nothing wrong with going fast and getting a lot done. But God also loves scuba diving. Scuba diving is a completely different experience. It is beneath the surface—slow and quiet. An entire world of beauty lies beneath the surface that you can't see when you are on the Jet Ski. God isn't asking you to choose either a Jet Ski or scuba gear. No! He wants a rhythm that includes both.

The word *Sabbath* is not a particularly deep or spiritual word. It simply means "to stop" or "to cease." The Lord anchors the command of Sabbath in creation. God essentially says, "In My creation of the universe I modeled for you this principle of rhythm. Work, then rest. Produce, then stop."

For in six days the LORD made the heavens, the earth, the sea, and everything in them; but on the seventh day he rested. That is why the LORD blessed the Sabbath day and set it apart as holy. (Exod. 20:11 NLT)

I love that verse 11 says God blessed the Sabbath day. It is not just holy and sacred; it is blessed. God infused the Sabbath day with blessings.

In Deuteronomy 5, the Ten Commandments are listed again. But this list includes a subtle change when the Lord talks about Sabbath.

Remember that you were once slaves in Egypt, but the LORD your God brought you out with his strong hand and powerful arm. That is why the LORD your God has commanded you to rest on the Sabbath day. (Deut. 5:15 NLT)

What does Sabbath keeping have to do with the Israelites' being slaves in Egypt? This verse actually contains a very powerful truth. Instead of anchoring Sabbath in creation, the Lord now anchors it in relationship. One thing that makes God's people different is that they stop. When they were slaves in Egypt, they had no days off, no rest, no vacation, and no downtime. But now as God delivers them and they are under His rulership and not the tyranny of Pharaoh, He wants them to know that rest is part of His divine design. There is an even deeper lesson God was wanting them to learn. Their value to Him was not just in what they could produce. Their value was in relationship. Let that sink in! Even when I am not working or producing on a Sabbath, I am just as valuable to God as when I am working. That is a lesson I have spent the last decade really trying to absorb and believe.

I can hear some of you saying, "Okay, I get it. The Sabbath made God's top ten list. But what does the New Testament teach about Sabbath? In fact, it seems like Jesus is always getting in trouble for violating the Sabbath."

The Jews had gone to great lengths to try to interpret the command of Sabbath. To help God out, they established all kinds of specific laws to define what was work and what wasn't work. When you read the stories found in the Gospels, Jesus wasn't violating the spirit of Sabbath but rather all these arbitrary rules the religious leaders had established.

And nowhere in the Gospels do we ever read that Jesus took the Ten Commandments down to the Nine Commandments.

The primary teaching of Jesus regarding the Sabbath is in Mark 2.

The Sabbath was made for man, not man for the Sabbath. (Mark 2:27)

Here is my loose paraphrase of Jesus's response: "God gave you the Sabbath as a gift. And you guys have totally messed this up. You took what God intended as a blessing and turned it into a religious burden."

If you think of the Sabbath as just another obligation you need to add to your schedule, you are missing Jesus's very point in Mark 2:27. Sabbath is not a "have to"; it is a "get to."

If you haven't done so already, I challenge you to study this for yourself. Take some time and work through the Bible passages on Sabbath.

If you don't have a biblical and theological conviction about the practice of Sabbath, the gravitational pull toward busyness will always win.

When I first started learning about Sabbath, it sounded like such a refreshing idea. However, as I have grown in my understanding of it, I have come to see that it is much more than a way to make sure you get the rest you need. I have come to believe that the practice of Sabbath is core to your spiritual formation, because it creates space for you to hear from and be with God.

Sabbath is one means of God ensuring that you get quality time with Him. If you are married, it's just like your relationship with your spouse. In the midst of a busy week you may have brief conversations, check in by phone during the day, or exchange text messages. It keeps you connected, but that is no substitute for unhurried, quality time together.

The following poem by Judy Brown beautifully illustrates the beauty and benefit of the gift of Sabbath.

Fire

What makes a fire burn
Is space between the logs,
A breathing space.
Too much of a good thing,
Too many logs
Packed in too tight
Can douse the flames
Almost as surely
As a pail of water.

So building fires
Requires attention
To the spaces in between
As much as to the wood.

64

When we are able to create
Open spaces in the same way
We have learned to pile on logs,
Then we come to see how
It is fuel, and the absence of fuel
That make fire possible.

We only need to lay on a log
Lightly from time to time.
A fire grows simply because the space is there,
With openings
in which the flame
that knows just how it wants to burn
can find its way.

Judy Brown[1]

I want to encourage you and your team to have a discussion about Sabbath. You might even consider as a team doing a Bible study on the topic. And then have some conversations with your teammates about the practical implications of observing it. How is Sabbath different from a day off? How can you support and encourage one another in your pursuit to have a rhythm that includes rest? Talk about ways you can help protect Sabbath for those on your team.

I also encourage you to talk about your team's rhythm. This is a great opportunity to look at your organizational calendar and evaluate the annual or seasonal rhythm. I know that in ministry there are times in the year when it is "all hands on deck." Everyone is putting in extra hours (it's Jet Ski time). That just comes with the territory. However, what I am advocating is that those intense ministry seasons be followed by celebration and rest. Most ministries I am around are not very good at celebrating or resting.

The Jews have a wonderful tradition that symbolizes the practical impact of Sabbath. It is called Havdalah. At the beginning of the Sabbath you light a candle, and that candle is a reminder that this day is different from the other six days. This is a day not about work and productivity but about rest and relationship (with God and with others). When the twenty-four hours of Sabbath are completed, the Jews take the candle and extinguish it in a cup of wine. And then they pour a little wine from the cup into a saucer. This symbolic act is to portray the truth that if you practice Sabbath well, it will spill over into the rest of your week and you will be a better person the other six days because you practiced Sabbath on the seventh day.

TEAM DISCUSSION QUESTIONS

1. Read back over "Fire" by Judy Brown. What word or phrase most stands out to you? Why?

2. What are your biggest roadblocks to consistently practicing Sabbath? As you answer that question, think about not only external circumstances but also internal roadblocks.

3. In Mark 2, Jesus says Sabbath is made for man. It is a gift meant to serve us. For you personally, what would be three benefits to practicing Sabbath? What would an ideal Sabbath day look like?

4. What steps could you take as a team to encourage one another personally in Sabbath keeping and in having a healthy organizational rhythm?

Please Like Me

I had just finished my sermon and walked off the platform. A pastor friend had asked me to speak at his church on the topic of prayer. This church had multiple services, so they provided a green room just off the platform where the speaker could hang out between services. As I was headed to the lobby to greet people, I stopped by the green room to leave my Bible and pick up a bottle of water. As I walked into the room, I picked up my phone and immediately noticed that I had a text message from someone. It wasn't somebody in my contacts because it showed only their phone number.

Now, remember that I had just finished my message about sixty seconds earlier—and all I could see on my home screen was the first line of this person's text message to me: "Weak and predictable." If you preach, you know that you take comments about your preaching very personally. In a nanosecond, I had this surge of insecurity wash over me. I had never had anyone so blatantly and directly tell me that my preaching was weak and predictable. Feelings of inadequacy and not being good enough rushed to the surface. When I opened the text message, it wasn't at all what I had thought it was. During my sermon, I had asked people to write down a word or two to describe their current prayer life, and this guy's two words were *weak* and *predictable*. Then he went on to thank me for the message and how it had been helpful to him. I remember thinking, *Couldn't you have started with the encouragement first, because now every insecurity in my body has been unleashed.*

I guess this issue of emotional health and separating my performance from my personhood is something I will be working on the rest of my days. I can relate to the words of Judith Hougen when she says, "We feel pulled to produce, to perform, to plow through the next five things on the to-do list. Our doing has become our being, and the untended garden of the inner life becomes overgrown with the tangled activities of an illusory person."[1]

I am struck by the words *our doing has become our being.* I can tell you from firsthand experience that living in such a way is unhealthy. When you find your worth in your position or the size of your church or your work ethic or your speaking ability or your latest achievement, you end up putting all your focus on the externals and neglecting your inner life. And it is a short hop from being performance driven to people pleaser. When you are driven by performance, part of the fuel for your ego and self-worth is that other people notice how much you are accomplishing. The need for affirmation, approval, and applause becomes a compelling force in your life. How you are perceived is everything.

This is not theory for me. This has been a daily battle. And my experience with ministry teams tells me it is a common struggle.

As David Benner says, "In all of creation, identity is a challenge only for humans."[2]

My wife and I have a dog named Baxter. He is pretty much the perfect dog; he doesn't shed, he rarely ever barks, and he is good with my four young granddaughters. He is extremely chill—just one notch above a stuffed animal.

In all the years we have had Baxter, we have never once had to send him to therapy or a counselor to talk about his issues of identity. We have never had to explore his family of origin. He is very comfortable in his own skin. There is no posturing, putting up a façade, or needing to prove himself. He is just comfortable being what he was created to be.

But for us humans, life is way more complex. As E. E. Cummings writes, "To be nobody-but-yourself in a world which is doing its best, night and day, to make you everybody but yourself—means to fight the hardest battle which any human being can fight—and never stop fighting."[3]

Being our authentic selves and staying real is one of the most courageous battles we'll ever fight.

From our earliest days on the planet, we have voices telling us who we should be and how we should be. Those voices have incredible power in our lives, especially during adolescence, and they begin to form the scripts we live by.

We quickly learn how to play the game in order to get the response and affirmation we want from people. Before long there is a widening gap between who we really are and the image we project that reflects who we think people want us to be.

A Latin phrase on an ancient coat of arms speaks to the tension we live with. It reads *Esse quam videri*, which means "to be rather than appear to be."

"What a long time it can take to become the person one has always been! How often in the process we mask ourselves in faces that are not our own."[4]

When you are not comfortable just being yourself, you put yourself under the control of other people. You cannot approve of yourself unless you get the fickle approval of others. You become an approval addict. And like any other addict, your addiction consumes your life and you can never get enough. It is like trying to fill a black hole. You were never made to find contentment and peace in the approval of others.

Okay—let's get really honest for a moment.

Behind our people pleasing is a deep fear that we will never be "enough."

For many of us in ministry, shame isn't about a sordid past or dark skeletons in our closet. It's that nagging sense deep in our guts that we don't measure up. It's the fear that our cover will be blown and people will finally discover "we are not all that and a bag of chips." And it leads to a lot of "un" feelings—unlovable, unworthy, undeserving, and undesirable.

Our sense of shame and inadequacy could come from old scripts from our family or a constantly critical spouse or a graceless church background or living in a culture that markets to our never being enough.

Lewis Smedes accurately describes shame when he writes, "The feeling of shame is about our very selves—not about some bad thing we did or said but about what we are. It tells us that we are unworthy. Totally. It is not as if a few seams in the garment of our selves need stitching; the whole fabric is frayed. We feel that we are unacceptable. And to feel that is a life-wearying heaviness."[5]

Wow! I know that is heavy stuff. But he is spot-on. You might need to spend some time alone with God and process this.

A Bible verse that every Christ-follower should have tattooed on their soul is Romans 8:1:

So now there is no condemnation for those who belong to Christ Jesus. (NLT)

None. Nada. Zero. Nil. There is not even a hint of condemnation for those who belong to Jesus. And when you let that truth seep deep down into your soul, you can no longer be held hostage to shame. You can now walk in freedom and grace.

This whole topic has huge implications for you personally as well as for how you do ministry and relate to your team.

When you are an approval addict, how does it manifest itself in your life and team?

1. Criticism and praise have more weight in your life than they deserve.

It has been said that for those of us in ministry, compliments are written in sand, but criticism is written in wet cement. That has certainly been true for me. I have carried disapproval deeply, and it takes a long time to dissipate and wear off. When I get that nasty email or someone attacks me on the internet, I so badly want to be able to blow it off. But those criticisms end up occupying more time and space in my thoughts than they deserve. When you find too much of your value in what others say and think, you end up working hard at being a diplomat and accommodating people to minimize criticism.

2. It will mess with your motives.

It's possible to do the right things for the wrong reasons. Instead of asking, "What's the right thing to do?" you are preoccupied by thoughts like *How will this make me look?* and *What will people think?*

It results in a lack of courage.

At times you won't say the right thing or do the right thing because you don't want the disapproval of others. Far too many times in my years of ministry, my fear of disapproval kept me from speaking up. But as people in ministry, we have a higher calling than the approval of people. And sometimes in order to please God you will have to displease and disappoint people.

In Galatians 1, Paul takes a courageous stand to protect the purity of the gospel. In verse 10, he writes, "Obviously, I'm not trying to win the approval of people, but of God. If pleasing people were my goal, I would not be Christ's servant" (NLT).

If you are going to courageously serve Christ, people pleasing cannot be your motive.

3. It will hijack your time and emotional energy.

On one hand, we spend too much emotional energy seeking people's affirmation. On the other, we spend way too much emotional energy worrying about criticism. Being a people pleaser is emotionally exhausting.

4. You won't receive criticism well.

When I am insecure and addicted to approval, I am unable to receive constructive criticism. What may be casual or normal feedback can feel devastating to a shame-prone person. If I am performance driven and you criticize my performance, it quickly feels like a personal attack.

Let's suppose you are sitting down with a team member to talk about a project you were having them work on. Then let's quantify the conversation. On a scale of 1–10, with 1 being neutral and nothing negative to say and 10 being a vicious attack, you give them feedback that feels to you like a 3. You've given them a couple of things they could have done differently, but in your mind, this is a mild level 3 conversation. To the person who struggles with shame, they receive the conversation as an 8.

As a people pleaser, I am unable to separate my performance from my person. So, I will deflect, blame, and justify.

5. You easily become defensive.

Defensiveness is a self-protecting mechanism to minimize shame and make the case that you are right and competent. When people start poking around on things that hit close to your sense of shame, the walls go up and the intensity rises.

6. You put the focus on yourself instead of others.

Paul gives a clear, straightforward command when he says:

> In humility value others above yourselves, not looking to your own interests but each of you to the interests of the others. (Phil. 2:3–4)

Here's the irony of being an approval addict. It really isn't at all about other people. It's purely about us.

When I was a kid, the neighborhood kids and I used to play flag football on our street. I loved it. But there was one part that I didn't love. It was the picking of teams. Usually a couple of the older boys were captains. Then the rest of us would line up and the two captains would start choosing people to be on their team. I was always cool and collected on the outside, but on the inside I was like a dog at the shelter wagging his tail, saying, "Pick me, pick me, pick me."

You may not be the biggest, best, brightest, or fastest—but God has picked you. I hope you never get over what it means that the God of the universe picked you. And just like Jesus, you are His dearly loved child.

When you can settle the identity question, you are in a place to do your best ministry. Because now you can bring your authentic self, not your shadow self or false self. Embracing your blessedness brings incredible freedom.

I love the words of Henri Nouwen when he writes, "The change of which I speak is the change from living life as a painful test to prove that you deserve to be loved, to living it as an unceasing 'Yes' to the truth of that Belovedness."[6]

One path is exhausting; the other is exhilarating. One path is life draining; the other is life giving. When this truth gets settled down in your soul, you can show up to your team each day without fear, willing to take the risk to just be yourself.

TEAM DISCUSSION QUESTIONS

1. When it comes to your team environment, what can make you feel insecure?

2. From the list of six ways that people pleasing can manifest itself, which one do you most need to take to heart?

3. In what ways can approval addiction show itself in a team setting?

4. What three words could be used to describe who you truly are—your "authentic self"?

PART 3

DEFINE
THE WIN

We live in a sensory-overloaded, opportunity-rich, option-excessive, attention-deficit culture. Your team's impact is directly linked to your ability to get crystal clear about priorities and then manage toward the desired results. In this section, we will explore how to remove the noise and distraction so you can become laser focused on your "must do's."

Management Matters

I love what the Willow Creek Global Leadership Summit has done to equip those of us in ministry to raise our leadership game. But one of my fears is that we have shined the spotlight so much on leadership that we have neglected the importance of good management. Can you imagine what would happen if it were announced that the Leadership Summit was going to become the Management Summit? I suspect that registration numbers would take a free fall. You certainly wouldn't need a seven-thousand-seat auditorium. Securing plenary session speakers might be a bit challenging as well. Finding exciting and inspiring management speakers is a little daunting. It also might be hard to find speakers for the Management Summit because these days no one wants to admit to being a manager.

I've been thinking about trying to rebrand and revitalize the word *management*. So I bought the web domain managementiscool.com.#leadership isoverrated. The truth is, management has gotten a bad rap over the last thirty years. Here are some popular quotes about management:

- "So much of what we call management consists in making it difficult for people to work." Peter Drucker

- "Management is doing things right, leadership is doing the right things." Peter Drucker[1]
- "Managers light a fire under people. . . . Leaders light a fire in people." Kathy Austin[2]
- "The manager maintains; the leader develops." Warren Bennis
- "The manager focuses on systems and structure; the leader focuses on people." Warren Bennis
- "The manager relies on control; the leader inspires trust." Warren Bennis[3]

No wonder no one wants to label themselves a manager. To get brutally honest, what we've been taught the last twenty-five years is that leaders are winners and managers are losers. And as a result of our focusing so much on leadership, at best management is characterized as a secondary gift.

It is time that we see management and leadership as complementary, not contradictory. We must value both. Michael Eisner, former CEO of Disney, was right when he said, "In every business, in every industry, management does matter."[4]

The following description helps depict how both leaders and managers add value and actually complement each other.

Leaders cast vision	Managers implement vision
Leaders define the destination	Managers build the road
Leaders live more in the future	Managers live more in the now
Leaders focus on the what/why	Managers focus on the how
Leaders emphasize the ends	Managers emphasize the means
Leaders provide inspiration	Managers deliver execution

Leadership and management are not mutually exclusive. Most of us have some leadership function in our roles as well as some management function. Very few of us have such a large organization that we can hand off all the management or leadership responsibility to someone else. I like the definition that says, "Management is the process of reaching organizational goals by working with and through people and other organizational resources."[5] Management is the ability to move the ball down the field. Managers get organizational traction.

This is what Master Sergeant Emil Zacharaia is referring to when he says, "You don't need anybody's permission to be a good leader, Lieutenant! All you have to do is be a resource to the team: know your people; look out after their welfare; keep them informed; let them take part in the decisions which affect them. Do this, and the team and you will succeed."[6]

A lot of what Zacharaia is describing is what I would call good management.

A great biblical story highlights the importance of management. It is found in Exodus 18 and is the story of Moses being the only leader and decision maker for two million people. Exodus 18 picks up when the Israelites had been liberated from Egypt and were on their way to the promised land. While Moses was on assignment from God to deliver the people from the bondage of Pharaoh, he decided to have his wife and two boys stay with her parents. Once Moses and the Israelites were safely out of Egypt, Jethro (Moses's father-in-law) brought Moses's wife and kids back to him.

> Moses told his father-in-law everything the Lord had done to Pharaoh and Egypt on behalf of Israel. He also told about all the hardships they had experienced along the way and how the Lord had rescued his people from all their troubles. Jethro was delighted when he heard about all the good things the Lord had done for Israel as he rescued them from the hand of the Egyptians. (Exod. 18:8–9 NLT)

The Israelites were in the middle of an amazing God story. They had witnessed miracle after miracle. It is mind-boggling what Moses and the people of Israel experienced.

The following day, Jethro went to work with Moses. It must have been bring-your-father-in-law-to-work day. The Bible says Moses took his seat and from morning until evening settled all the disputes. He was the only judge—for more than two million people. Think of all the wasted time spent waiting in line to get a few minutes with Moses. It must have been worse than the DMV office.

It had to have been stressful, frustrating, and exhausting for the people. But it was no party for Moses either—think of how he must have felt. He would drop into bed day after day, exhausted and drained. Then he would get up early, scarf down a bowl of cereal, and head to the office. And when he pulled into the parking lot, a long line of people who needed something from him was already forming.

Any dispute that could not be settled was brought to Moses, no matter how small or big. When Jethro watched this for a day, he said to Moses, "What is this you are doing for the people? Why do you alone sit as judge, while all these people stand around you from morning till evening?" (Exod. 18:14). That's a nice way of asking, "Have you lost your mind?" It was like Moses being the solo judge for the entire metro area of Austin, Texas.

Listen to Moses's response: he said he does this "because the people come to me to seek God's will" (v. 15). Translation: "They need me." It's like Moses was saying, "That's just how we roll here. There are a lot of needy people, and I can't turn them away. So I just stay at it and work hard until everyone gets what they need from me."

This sounds like a conversation I've had many times with my wife, Connie. She would look at the pace of my life and how I was doing ministry and basically say, "This is nuts." I would respond with statements like, "I'm a pastor." "I'm needed." "This just comes with being in ministry." "I can't say no." And like Moses, I found myself in an unhealthy and unsustainable way of life.

What Moses was oblivious to, Jethro saw as obvious. Jethro responds, "What you are doing is not good. You and these people who come to you will only wear yourselves out" (vv. 17–18). Basically, he says, "You have a broken management system." The current system was ineffective, exhausting, and dysfunctional. It was wasting time and energy. Moses was the bottleneck. This system was wearing out Moses *and* the people. When we have poorly devised and poorly functioning management systems, we will wear out ourselves and our teams. We will end up spending a lot of sideways energy managing the problems of a broken system.

As an outsider, Jethro could see things more clearly and objectively. By the way, when you have a broken management system, the answer isn't to just work harder. But that's usually our go-to response. I love that Moses listened to his father-in-law. He was teachable. He didn't blow up or become defensive. He didn't pull the position card. Even though the way Moses was leading had to be exhausting, it can really stroke your ego. "I'm the man. I'm the woman! When people have a problem, they come to me."

When Jethro asked, "Why do you do all this alone?" I think he was putting his finger on a very important principle of Scripture. No one is gifted enough to do it all alone. No one has all the gifts. That's the beauty of the body of Christ. It's about all of us using our gifts. And we need both gifted leaders and effective managers.

It takes a team to effectively lead the church, not just a couple of gifted superstars. When Jethro offers Moses some advice for solving this dilemma, he points out the need for managers and a management system. "But select capable men from all the people—men who fear God, trustworthy men who hate dishonest gain—and appoint them as officials over thousands, hundreds, fifties and tens" (v. 21). Jethro is encouraging Moses to find some men of high competency and high character to help manage the load. He is also advocating a management system that could be effective and better spread out the load.

I believe it is significant that Moses started with the people first and then addressed the issue of a system. If you have highly competent managers with high characters, they can figure out the management systems. However, you can have fabulous systems, but if your managers aren't competent, they will never execute the systems effectively.

I love the hopeful words of Jethro in verse 23: "If you do this and God so commands, you will be able to stand the strain, and all these people will go home satisfied." This was a win-win. It was a win for Moses in that he wouldn't burn out. It was a win for the people because their problems could be resolved in a more timely and effective manner. And that was largely because competent managers were appointed and a management system was implemented.

Let me say it again . . . management matters! It really does. If you have a management role in your organization, wear your label proudly. It is not a secondary gift. A leader without managers is like a quarterback without an offensive line. The offensive line does the hard work down in the trenches and creates the path for the ball to move forward.

TEAM DISCUSSION QUESTIONS

1. In your opinion, what are the top three qualities of a great manager?

2. Part of management is about having good systems. Do you think your team has strong systems? Do you think your organization has strong systems? Explain.

3. Much of Moses's problem was that he was carrying too much of a load. Are you currently carrying something that could be delegated to someone else?

4. Most all of us have to do some management as part of our role. What is one area where you could improve your management?

10

"Squirrel"

They say that confession is good for the soul. And I'm all about having a good soul, so I should probably make a confession. Today as I was trying to write this chapter on priority and focus, I was having a hard time staying focused. I found myself repeatedly sidetracked by every imaginable distraction—checking email, reading text messages, getting a snack, watching the news, taking phone calls, removing a splinter in my finger, booking airline tickets, making dinner plans, etc.

The truth is, staying on task these days seems to be an almost insurmountable undertaking. We are a distractible people living in a distractible world.

It reminds me of a scene from the movie *Up*. Dug the dog is talking to Carl, the old man, and out of nowhere Dug's head spins and he yells, "Squirrel!" It seems like all day every day, "squirrels" take our focus off what we are trying to do.

An ancient Chinese proverb says, "The eagle that chases two rabbits at one time will catch neither." However, in the twenty-first century, it is more like chasing twenty rabbits at once.

All our techno-gadgets and the incessant bombardment of sound bites into our lives has conditioned us to have very short attention spans. *Squirrel!* Just seeing if you were still with me. Much about life and ministry today makes it difficult to establish priorities and stay focused on those priorities, if we even know what our priorities should be.

It's like the old saying "You can do almost anything you want, but you just can't do everything you want." There will always be more good ideas than there are time, energy, and capacity to chase after them.

Life is about choices. Choices about priorities. It's about choosing best over good, important over urgent, eternal over temporal, and essential over trivial. In his book *Boundaries for Leaders*, Henry Cloud talks about "being ridiculously in charge."[1] We have to regularly remind ourselves that we are ridiculously in charge of our one and only life. If we don't prioritize our life and ministry, I promise that somebody else will be glad to do it for us. Everybody has an opinion on how we should spend our time.

In this chapter, I want specifically to talk about establishing and focusing on the priorities in your ministry and team. We all know that diffused light can barely light up a room, but concentrated light can cut through a steel beam. And in the same way, diffused and scattered focus ends up being ineffective, but concentrated and laser focus has exponential power.

None of us like the feeling of spinning our wheels or being stuck. We like the feeling of traction and progress. There is something fulfilling about the feeling of forward movement.

I live in Colorado, and it is not unusual in the winter for people to get their cars stuck in the snow. And when you get stuck, your first instinct is to give it the gas. Surely more fuel and more effort is the solution. Your wheels start spinning faster, but you can't get any traction and usually get yourself into a deeper hole. Eventually, you get out of your vehicle and examine the situation. You need to take a careful look at what's causing you to be stuck before you can figure out the best solution.

The same is true with your ministry life. It is helpful to assess the things that get in the way of focusing on your priorities.

What Gets in the Way . . .

Organizational Gnats

A senior executive with a home improvement retailer once said, "We don't have dragons swooping down and knocking us off our priorities. What we have are gnats."[2]

What gets us off track is usually not laziness or carelessness but rather busyness. It's the little organizational "squirrels" that cause us to lose sight of our priorities. There are meetings to attend, emails to return, calls to make, problems to solve. And sometimes those things have nothing to do with our most important priorities. I realize that some things we can't say no to—they are just part of serving in an organization. But sometimes we can get caught up in the fast-moving current of a ministry and never really evaluate whether all our activities are serving our highest priorities.

Shiny New Opportunities

Most people in ministry are not in danger of being addicted to cocaine or alcohol, but we can easily be addicted to adrenaline. And chasing after more, more, more can be an adrenaline rush—especially when we are chasing after more in Jesus's name. But chasing after the newest, shiniest, sexiest idea may not need to be our highest priority. I fear that at times new vision is cast simply because the leader is bored with the old vision. Sometimes it is the new . . . *squirrel!* . . . that distracts us from what should be our core priorities.

As Steve Jobs said, "People think focus means saying yes to the thing you've got to focus on. But that's not what it means at all. It means saying no to the hundred other good ideas that there are."[3]

In healthy churches and ministries, time is spent in prayer and listening to the voice of God to discern what to pursue.

Do you remember that classic line from the 1993 movie *Jurassic Park*, when Jeff Goldblum's character says the scientists were so preoccupied with whether they could that they never stopped to think if they should? In ministry, what takes us from could to should is the discernment of God's voice and direction.

FOMO

FOMO is, of course, the fear of missing out. What I mean by this is that we can waste enormous time because we want to be in on the text thread with the group. We can attend a conference just to hang out with a group of ministry friends and those three days don't do anything to move our ministry priorities forward. Or we can waste significant time engaging social media because we don't want to miss out on the latest trend or piece of news. And social media can promote this illusion that everybody is having more adventure than us, taking more exotic vacations than us, hanging out with more interesting people than us, and changing the world more than us. And it just fuels our FOMO and takes our eyes off of our priorities. So, my challenge to you is this: just say *no* to FOMO.

Urgent vs. Important

In the words of John Maxwell, "You cannot overestimate the unimportance of practically everything."[4] For so many years in ministry, I had a theology of availability. If someone had a need, I was to be available. If there was a problem, I should be available. If someone had a pressing issue, it became my pressing issue. I know there are divine interruptions, and I want to be sensitive to the God moments that cross my path. But constant availability undermined my priorities. When I think about how Jesus lived His life, He always seemed to march to the beat of His Father's voice. When people tried to pull or sway or coerce Him, He stayed the course. Every time He walked out of a town, there were still more people to heal, demons to cast out, and miracles to work. But He still left, because He had a sense of priority that transcended the urgent requests of those around Him. He was very clear about what was most important and refused to let the chirping of the urgent derail Him.

To Do vs. Must Do

It has taken me years to learn this, but there is a huge difference between a to-do list and a must-do list.

To-Do List	Must-Do List
Reactive	Proactive
Random	Thoughtful
Long	Short
Trivial	Vital
Everything appears equal	Ranked by importance
False sense of accomplishment	Fulfilling sense of accomplishment
Short-term impact	Long-term impact

I'm sure you have never done this, but here is something I would commonly do in the past. I would create my to-do list and then throughout the day I would review it and check off the things I had accomplished. Then I would think about something I did that day that wasn't on my to-do list. Being the sicko that I am, I would add that task to the list just so I could check off another box. It wasn't a sign of progress on my priorities. It was probably more of a sign that I needed counseling. Don't get trapped in the "check box" game.

Work Harder vs. Work Smarter

Because I have valued productivity, hard work, and being busy for most of my ministry, I have found very little space for reflection, processing, evaluating, and discerning. "Always look busy" has been my mantra. When I would come up against a wall, my strategy was just to put my shoulder down and bust through the wall. I figured the path to success was a road called "hard work." What I discovered is that you can have a really strong work ethic but not be working on the most important things.

Not long ago Connie and I partnered with some friends and bought a cabin property in the mountains. Fifteen years ago in the area where we purchased the property, a woman who actually worked for the US Forest Service was trying to burn a letter from her estranged husband and caused a massive forest fire called the Hayman Fire.

Over six hundred structures were destroyed, over five thousand people were evacuated, over 137,000 acres were burned, and over $40 million was spent fighting the fire.

Well, as a result, our property contained a good number of burned and downed trees. Recently my friend and I started clearing out and burning the dead trees. A number of trees twenty to thirty feet in length were left lying in a ravine just a few yards from our cabin. We stood on a slope and used a chainsaw to cut these large trees. Then, once they had been cut into six- to eight-foot sections, we had to roll them down the hill to a flat spot where we could burn them. It was hard and exhausting work.

Then my friend, during a break, took a few minutes and thought about a way to work smarter. He had the idea to tie a rope on these big trees and pull them down to a flat area to cut them with the chainsaw near where we were burning the logs. It was much safer and at least 50 percent easier.

It is amazing that just a little bit of thinking time resulted in a much more effective and productive strategy.

Sometimes the answer isn't just to work harder. We regularly need thinking and reflection time to gain clarity not just about what our priorities are but also about how we can most effectively execute them.

Unwillingness to Disappoint People

To focus on our highest priorities means we will have to learn to say no to some good requests and urgent demands. That is difficult for those of us in ministry. We are the "yes people," not the "no people." Effective leaders and effective teams learn the discipline of saying no.

Tony Blair, former prime minister of Great Britain, once said, "The art of leadership is saying no, not saying yes. It is very easy to say yes."[5]

Here is where it gets tricky for those of us in ministry. Saying no means we have to be okay with disappointing people. If I am an approval addict, I will always have a hard time staying focused on my priorities. Therefore, this is really an emotional health issue that I have to own for myself. The real problem is not with the other person making the request. The problem is with my misdirected thinking. The problem is with my finding too much of my identity and worth in everyone else's opinion of me. I am trying to learn to shift my perspective. Instead of focusing on the fact I am saying no to somebody or something, I try to focus on the fact that I am saying yes to the things that matter most.

As I close this chapter, let me leave you with this question: What squirrels do you need to get rid of so you can focus on your priorities?

TEAM DISCUSSION QUESTIONS

1. Which one of the following most gets in your way when it comes to focusing on your priorities? Explain.

Organizational Gnats
Shiny New Opportunities

FOMO
Urgent vs. Important
To Do vs. Must Do
Work Harder vs. Work Smarter
Unwillingness to Disappoint People

2. What are the three most annoying organizational gnats that derail you from your priorities?
3. What is one distraction you can eliminate so you can focus on your priorities?
4. What could you do as a team to minimize distractions and help one another focus on key priorities?

11

What Does Success Look Like?

A job description is not a priority list. That is a bit of an overstatement, because a good job description should inform your priorities and where you're going to focus your time. I see most job descriptions as a general and broad list of objectives. A good job description should define the win of the position. But a job description doesn't define how you're going to accomplish those objectives or which objective is most important right now. And a job description doesn't define how you're going to utilize your time to accomplish the objectives.

In my experience, a job description is more a hiring tool than a priority or management tool. Let me prove it to you. When was the last time you looked at your job description? I suspect most of us would have a hard time even finding our job description. And a percentage of us never even got one.

Priorities are value judgments. For example, creating a volunteer development strategy is more important right now than planning next summer's student camp. Your short-term priorities should create progress toward the accomplishment of your long-term objectives.

Once you know the "win" for your role, the next step is to gain clarity around your short-term priorities that move toward that defined win. That sounds straightforward and simple, but it is easy to fall into a weekly routine of activity—prepare a message, lead staff meeting, counsel, solve problems, fill out reports . . . rinse and repeat. You can go weeks and months without really evaluating whether you are focused on the right priorities.

Two Questions to Consider

1. What's the win of your position?

In principle, the highest level of performance always comes from people who are emotionally engaged, and the highest level of engagement comes from those who know the score—that is, if people know whether they are winning or losing.[1]

One exercise I like to lead staff teams through is to have everyone write a one-sentence job description. I think one reason we never go back to our job descriptions is that they are too long and too broad. But if you had to define the win of your position, what would it be? I challenge you to give that some serious thought and take the time to carefully craft a one-sentence job description. Once you have written it out, I recommend you sit down with your supervisor and see if they agree with your definition of the "win."

2. What are your top three priorities over the next thirty days?

That question forces me to make a value judgment, rank my priorities, and define what's most important. When I am driven by tasks rather than priorities, everything feels equally important: everything is just a check box on my to-do list.

In *Scrum*, a book on organizational effectiveness, Jeff Sutherland writes, "When I go into a company, I usually find that about 85 percent of effort is wasted. Only a sixth of any of the work done actually produces something of value."[2]

Apparently there is a systemic problem with people not focusing on and executing that which is most important.

Not long ago I did an exercise with a staff team where I had everyone write down their top three priorities. A few days later I got an email from a supervisor who was there that day. He wrote out what he thought the top three priorities should be for each staff member he supervised. Then he sat down with each person and compared his list with theirs. In his email, he said he was shocked by how different their lists were. Without intentionality in defining priorities, misalignment is a sure result. And when there is misalignment, there is wasted energy, poor stewardship of resources, and lost opportunity.

Three Strategies to Implement

Let me share with you some strategies to make sure you are clear about your priorities. In organizations, clarity is always a friend.

Block time for reflection and thinking.

The weekly grind of ministry responsibility can keep you from achieving clarity about priorities. It is the difference between a ground view and an aerial view. When you are on the ground, you can only see what's right around you. You have a micro view instead of a macro view. A ground view is great for seeing details, but only an aerial view can provide a big-picture perspective. It is the difference between what you can see walking down the street versus what you can see sitting in an airplane at thirty thousand feet.

You need to regularly pull back and up so you can get an aerial view of your ministry. Let me give you an example. Doing a training session for small group leaders this Thursday night is a ground view. But an aerial view would be to step back and ask questions such as:

- What is our philosophy of small group leader training?
- What is the profile for an equipped and developed small group leader?
- What is the win for our training?
- Who else can we learn from about training small group leaders?
- What is the best delivery system for our training?

The aerial view always needs to inform and drive the ground view. That's the way it works in the military. The aerial surveillance view informs where the ground troops need to go. The ministry equivalent of aerial surveillance would be think time, prayer, strategic conversation, and reflection. I know it is counterintuitive, but the faster, bigger, and busier the ministry, the more you need dedicated space to think, reflect, and hear God.

Define the wildly important.

I like the phrase "wildly important," which comes from the book *The 4 Disciplines of Execution*. It draws me to ask questions such as:

- What catapults us toward accomplishing our vision?
- What will bring God the most glory?
- What will produce the most kingdom fruit?
- What will bring exponential results?
- What will result in true spiritual impact?

Defining the wildly important is about sifting through all that you could do and identifying what you must do, clarifying what you are going to go big on. Without absolute clarity on the wildly important, you will have misdirected and diffused focus—and you will never reach your kingdom potential.

It might be helpful to think of all your activities as money. For example, sending an email might be a one-dollar task. Sitting in a meeting might be a twenty-dollar return. Brainstorming a better ministry strategy might be a one-thousand-dollar payoff. But on a to-do list, they all look as though they have the same importance. They are just tasks to be checked off.

By the way, this is not something you do once and then you're done. This is something you must continually revisit. Visions change. Strategies change. Organizations change. Communities change. In other words, what might have been wildly important a year ago may not be today.

Without continually clarifying priorities, mission drift and wasted effort are guaranteed. "One prime suspect behind execution breakdown was clarity of objective: People simply didn't understand the goal they were supposed to execute. In fact, in our initial surveys we learned that only one employee in seven could name even one of their organization's most important goals."[3]

Clarity must start at the top and then trickle down. Once senior leadership has clearly defined and articulated the goal/vision, then you can know how to align your priorities to help your team see the vision fulfilled. If you are not in senior leadership, I encourage you to consistently engage your supervisor regarding your priorities. Seek them out and make sure the two of you agree on your core priorities.

Narrow the focus.

"It is those who concentrate on but one thing at a time who advance this world."[4]

That is a statement about focus and priority.

What if you spent 70 percent of your time on your three highest priorities? Think of the potential fruit and impact. What would it take for that to happen? What would you have to delegate or eliminate to free up bandwidth?

"Focus on the wildly important requires you to go against your basic wiring as a leader and focus on less so that your team can achieve more."[5]

I like the fact that *The 4 Disciplines of Execution* talks about the wildly *important*. Not the wildly trendy or wildly creative or wildly shiny or wildly popular or wildly innovative. Because you are in ministry, you are called to pursue the biblically and eternally important. This, of course, requires doing the hard work of defining what is wildly important for you as a ministry and a team.

Defining your priorities is what Stephen Covey calls putting first things first.[6]

To demonstrate this, he uses what has become a well-known illustration, but it is even more relevant now for those of us doing ministry in the twenty-first century.

Imagine the time you give to your ministry as a bucket. The bucket has only so much capacity; it has limits. And you have limits regarding the time you can give to your ministry. The bucket has the ability to hold a lot of different things. You have many options for what you could put in your ministry bucket.

If you are like most people in ministry, your bucket is full. But do you have room in your bucket for your highest priorities? This assumes you know what those highest priorities are. The main point of Covey's illustration is that you have to put in the big rocks first. If your bucket is filled with the pebbles of random activity or the small rocks of meaningless meetings, no room is left for the big rocks of core priorities.

In this season, what are your core priorities? What is wildly important for your ministry? What is wildly important for your specific team? What is wildly important for your role on the team?

As Greg McKeown writes in *Essentialism*, "Anyone can talk about the importance of focusing on the things that matter most—and many people do—but to see people who dare to live it is rare."[7]

TEAM DISCUSSION QUESTIONS

1. What is your one-sentence job description?
2. What is your one (or two at the most) wildly important goal?
3. How important is reflection and think time for you and your role? How much and how often do you need this?
4. What would have to change so that you could give 70 percent of your time to your highest priorities?

12

The Word Nobody Likes but Everybody Needs

A couple of years ago I had the chance to sit down with a former staff member who had served on my team more than a decade earlier. We hadn't kept in touch very much, but we had a great lunch together as we reminisced and shared stories about our years together on a church staff. Then at one point during our lunch, the conversation turned more serious. In a moment of candor, he said to me, "You know, you weren't very easy to work for." And then he spent a little time sharing specific ways that I had been difficult to work for. He was kind, but it was definitely a rebuke of how I led at times.

At first, I could feel myself wanting to be defensive, to explain, to rationalize, or to share ways he had been difficult as well. Those feelings quickly took me to a dark place I was very familiar with: a place of insecurity and inadequacy. Not feeling "good enough" has been an unwelcome companion for much of my ministry.

In recent years I have done some hard work on my performance and identity issues. Rather than try to defend myself, I was able to be present and really listen to him. And the truth is, he was right. As an ambitious, driven leader, I could sometimes run over people. Because of how I led,

96

I'm sure it never felt safe to have this conversation when I was his boss. Even though it was years later, my friend was holding me accountable for my actions.

Accountability—it's an uncomfortable word, isn't it? It doesn't evoke a warm, fuzzy feeling when you hear it. In fact, it has the same emotional warmth as the word *colonoscopy*. Accountability often seems to imply a problem, a sin, a shortcoming, a lack of follow-through, a dropping of the ball. No one ever has an accountability conversation to tell you how amazing you are. But even though such conversations are uncomfortable, they are absolutely necessary to our growth, both personally and professionally.

When Accountability Goes Missing

Because those of us in ministry usually avoid uncomfortable conversations like the plague, holding people accountable doesn't come easy for us. But when accountability is lacking, it has at least three negative implications.

1. We don't get the desired results.

If we are called by God and have a divine assignment from God, then results matter. It is a stewardship issue. As an organization we have been entrusted with money, time, people, and skills; not maximizing those resources for kingdom impact is poor stewardship. "An organization becomes comfortably stuck in a culture of non-performance. It becomes an open secret that goal setting is nothing more than a meaningless paper exercise. People learn acceptable organizational excuses for explaining why they didn't achieve their goals."[1]

Our terminal "niceness" keeps us from addressing what we know to be true and real. And the result is a culture of non-performance. Some leaders will talk about having a "hands-off" or an empowering style of leadership. For some, that is code for "I am unwilling to confront the issues of non-performance." Of course, we want to empower people to succeed. But there is a difference between empowering people and abdicating our own leadership responsibility to get the desired results.

2. Lack of accountability perpetuates dysfunction.

Accountability is not just about performance and results. It is also an emotional health and team health issue. Lack of accountability can lead to a toxic culture. Because of our unwillingness to have hard conversations, we tolerate dysfunctional and destructive behavior.

In Galatians 2, Paul holds Peter, who had fallen into a behavior that was dysfunctional and wrong, accountable. "But when Peter came to Antioch, I had to oppose him to his face, for what he did was very wrong. When he first arrived, he ate with the Gentile believers, who were not circumcised. But afterward, when some friends of James came, Peter wouldn't eat with the Gentiles anymore. He was afraid of criticism from these people who insisted on the necessity of circumcision. As a result, other Jewish believers followed Peter's hypocrisy, and even Barnabas was led astray by their hypocrisy" (Gal. 2:11–13 NLT).

This is such a powerful example. Can you imagine how it must have felt for Paul to challenge Peter? Peter was one of the original twelve disciples and in Jesus's inner circle. But Paul had the courage to oppose him to his face. He didn't talk *about* Peter; he talked *to* him.

Notice that verse 11 says what Peter did was "very wrong." Sometimes accountability is about lack of follow-through or missing a deadline. But sometimes it is about unhealthy and inappropriate behavior. Certainly, if Peter was susceptible to dysfunctional behavior, so are you and I.

We learn from this passage that dysfunction always has a ripple effect. Verse 13 tells us that Peter's hypocrisy rubbed off on Barnabas and other Jewish believers. If it had gone unaddressed, this dysfunction had the potential of being divisive to the early church and taking them "off task."

3. Lack of accountability limits people's personal growth.

If we authentically care about those who serve on our teams, we will do what is best for them even when it is uncomfortable for us. According to author Patrick Lencioni,

> Many leaders who struggle with this will try to convince themselves that their reluctance is a product of their kindness; they just don't want to make their employees (or team members) feel bad. But an honest reassessment of

their motivation will allow them to admit that they are the ones who don't want to feel bad and that failing to hold someone accountable is ultimately an act of selfishness.[2]

Ouch! Lencioni is spot-on. If I am honest, my unwillingness to hold people accountable is actually about me. I don't want to be the "bad guy." I don't want the person to think poorly of me. I don't want the discomfort of a hard conversation.

Some people who have twenty years of ministry experience don't really have twenty years of experience. They have one year of experience repeated twenty times. They have never really developed and grown much. And sometimes a lack of accountability has resulted in their stunted growth. Let me say it directly: we are not helping people when we don't hold them accountable.

When we really stop and reflect on it, the issue of accountability is both internal and external. It is about internal attitude and external organizational practices.

Internal Attitude

As we have talked about several times, team health begins with personal health.

I need to learn to see accountability as good and necessary for my growth. You see, accountability will help close the gap between who I say I want to be and who I actually am today.

Here's the truth. I am gloriously saved and on my way to heaven. Even though I am in the process of being "sanctified," I can still behave in dysfunctional ways and drop the ball organizationally. I have blind spots. I am insecure. I have bad days. I can lack self-awareness. I have rough edges and broken places from my past.

God uses people and their words to shine a light on our blind spots and smooth out some of our rough edges. God uses the authority of my supervisor to sharpen me and help me grow. And if I am going to become like Jesus, I need a handful of people in my life who can tell me what I need to hear, not just what I want to hear.

I am not talking about a person who is a verbal wrecking ball. There is definitely an unhealthy way to hold people accountable. I'm talking about having an internal attitude of openness to receive healthy accountability. It takes courage and a healthy identity in Christ to welcome accountability.

When you study the book of Proverbs, you discover that words such as *rebuke*, *discipline*, and *correction* are almost always seen as a gift.

> People who accept discipline are on the pathway to life,
> but those who ignore correction will go astray. (Prov. 10:17 NLT)

> An open rebuke
> is better than hidden love!
> Wounds from a sincere friend
> are better than many kisses from an enemy. (Prov. 27:5–6 NLT)

Here is an important question for every person in ministry to honestly answer: "Who in your life can rebuke you?" Leaning in when it comes to accountability will serve you well not only personally but also in your ministry environment.

Organizational Practice

In an international survey of hundreds of business and government agencies, "A staggering 81 percent of the people surveyed said they were not held accountable for regular progress on the organization's goals. . . . In short, people weren't sure what the goal was, weren't committed to it, didn't know what to do about it specifically, and weren't held accountable for it."[3]

No wonder so many organizations and ministries are stuck in nonperformance. A discussion about accountability in a ministry presumes that there is clarity around vision and priorities.

If you are a team leader or supervisor and you are removing organizational roadblocks as well as supporting and resourcing your people, it is a reasonable expectation that they are making progress and getting their jobs done. If you are authentically caring for them and celebrating their wins, it is appropriate to hold people accountable for the agreed-upon results.

One reason the word *accountability* gets a bad rap is because of the way some people have carried out accountability. Holding people accountable does not mean using your position as an excuse to embarrass, humiliate, mistreat, belittle, or shame people. Your accountability of people should make them better not bitter.

"How" you hold people accountable is key. You must be direct enough to be clear but gracious enough to create openness. You must care about the results and the relationship. Accountability has a direct correlation to trust. When you trust and believe someone is "for you," then you are much more willing to receive the hard conversation. Making relational deposits makes having hard conversations about performance and progress much easier.

Accountability must always model truth and grace. It should come from genuine concern for the individual and the ministry, not from a place of anger or frustration.

By the way, your words really matter when it comes to accountability conversations. Learn to use phrases that are not accusatory—phrases such as:

- "I notice . . ."
- "My observation is . . ."
- "My concern is . . ."
- "Can you help me understand?"
- "I'd like for us to have a conversation about . . ."

What about the times when you are on the receiving end of an accountability conversation? You must do the hard work on your own personal emotional health so that accountability conversations don't send you to a dark place. The two biggest indicators that I have gone to a dark place are either defensiveness or defeat. Both responses make the conversation more about personhood than performance. And both are driven by insecurity. And when defensiveness and defeat take over, it is next to impossible to have a healthy conversation about performance.

Practical Challenges

1. Stay humble and teachable.

None of us have our acts together completely. We all blow it. We all make mistakes. We all drop the ball occasionally. Welcome to the human race. Some of us in ministry need to give ourselves permission to just be human.

2. See accountability as an opportunity to get better.

Healthy accountability makes us better. Generally speaking, we are on our game a little more when we know people are watching. I am not an avid cyclist, but I do have a bike that I enjoy riding. When I am riding and no one is around, I will just coast and take a breather—until I see another bike coming my way. Then I start pedaling fast and furious. Something about being watched pushes us to do more than we would do if we weren't being watched.

3. Invite accountability.

I know some of us have had a bad experience with accountability, and we are a little gun-shy. I get it. But just because you had a bad meal at a restaurant doesn't mean you stop eating. Let your boss know you want to be accountable. Let them know you care about getting better, not just in your performance but also in how you interact with the team.

4. Consider the stakes.

Much is at stake for you personally and for the ministry you serve. The higher up you go in ministry, the more diligently you have to work at pursuing accountability. The higher your position on the org chart, the more people are apt to put you on a pedestal and let you live in isolation. In fact, I often tell senior leaders, "You don't just need to give a few people permission to speak into your life; you need to give them a sense of responsibility. You need to say to a couple of people, 'There is too much at stake in my life for me to blow it. If you see something going on that needs to be addressed, you have to come to me. I need you to protect me from myself.'" Lack of accountability can lead to stuck ministries, unhealthy cultures, sin, unrealized potential, and squandered opportunities.

So, lean in. You and your team will be better for it.

TEAM DISCUSSION QUESTIONS

1. Honestly, how well do you "lean in" when it comes to receiving accountability?

2. How can lack of accountability perpetuate dysfunction?

3. Do you have anybody in your life who can rebuke you? You need to give them not only permission but also a sense of responsibility to speak into your life.

4. Of the practical applications below, which one do you need to embrace?

  ☐ Stay humble and teachable.

  ☐ See accountability as an opportunity to get better.

  ☐ Invite accountability.

  ☐ Consider the stakes.

13

The Team Equivalent
of an IRS Audit

L et me state the obvious. Everybody hates performance reviews. And I
mean everybody. Well, maybe the one exception would be HR directors.
But supervisors generally don't like them. And employees tend to despise
them. Most performance reviews feel like an IRS audit. You never quite
know what to expect, but you know it's not going to be fun. It's stressful
and unnerving and usually worse than you anticipated. One journalist calls
it "the annual ritual of fear and loathing."[1]

It would be one thing if performance reviews were painful but helpful, like
passing a kidney stone. But when it is the double whammy of painful and
unproductive, you start to question why you have to go through it. In churches,
nonprofits, and businesses, leaders have started questioning the conventional
approach to performance evaluation. In a recent study, only 4 percent of HR
managers think their system of assessing employees is effective at measuring
performance—and 83 percent say their systems need an overhaul.[2]

There is a growing consensus in organizations that the old-school approach to performance evaluation is counterproductive. A variety of reasons
are causing organizations to jettison the old approach and look for more
effective ways to assess their employees:

- A year's worth of performance issues that are bundled together and downloaded at an annual review is less helpful than real-time feedback about current performance.
- An annual review feels too weighty. An entire year's worth of work and effort is loaded into a single evaluation. Most of us would rather get hit by a snowball every week than by an avalanche once a year.
- The speed of life and ministry makes an annual review too little, too late.
- An annual review feels more organizational than personal. It is formal, not informal. In most organizations I've worked with, the performance evaluation process was something people were obligated to get done rather than a meaningful resource that really helped the organization's mission and the people being evaluated.
- It feels like your fourth-grade report card from Mrs. Singleton. I remember getting an *I* (improvement needed) in handwriting on my fourth-grade report card. Looking back, I see Mrs. Singleton was actually being gracious in giving me an *I*. I don't remember any other grade I got that semester, but I do remember that one. I had no idea my handwriting was subpar until my report card came out. I felt ambushed. I was surprised and distraught to see such a poor mark. That happens a lot in performance reviews. There will have been no discussion of performance issues throughout the year, and then something is brought up during the annual review. And just like me in the fourth grade, the team member walks away surprised and frustrated.
- The review has been heavily weighted on grading past performance with too little attention given to proactively discussing how to improve current and future performance.

To read the last several paragraphs, you might think I am down on evaluating performance. Not at all! I am for the "wine" of real-time, honest feedback. What I am not a fan of is the "wineskin" of a once-a-year report card. I am on a mission to do away with the Mrs. Singleton moments.

I do believe productive evaluation can be helpful for everyone's development and growth. I also believe people want to do a good job, and along the way they want to receive helpful feedback. American executive and businessman Jack Welch is a big fan of letting people know how they are doing. In a *Wall Street Journal* commentary, he said, "As a manager, you owe candor to your people."[3] Candor, sprinkled with grace, is healthy and preserves dignity.

A large percentage of churches and ministry organizations choose not to do any kind of performance reviews. The problem is that years can go by without any productive assessment of how the person is performing or ways they can grow and improve. That is unfair to them and poor stewardship of the organization's mission and resources.

Or worse, nothing is ever communicated to an underperforming staff member, and then they are called to a meeting and let go from the team. They are shocked, confused, and devastated—and their feelings are valid. When a person has to be released from their position, it should never be a surprise. And it should never happen without the person already knowing exactly where they stand and having had a chance to turn their performance around.

While a lot of ministry organizations don't do any kind of performance evaluation, those ministry organizations that do them often do them out of obligation, fear of legal consequence, and a sense that they are a necessary evil. In these churches, performance reviews feel much like a root canal. You put it off as long as you possibly can, and then you grudgingly submit to the painful process.

It is a new day, and we need a new way. We need a new plan for not only evaluating current performance but also fueling improved performance.

I would advocate a process that is

- more personal, less organizational;
- more informal, less formal;

and contains

- more coaching, less grading;
- more dialogue, less monologue.

I believe the better approach is to have regular conversations rather than an annual evaluation.

Deloitte, one of the largest service organizations in the world, has been doing a major overhaul of how they assess performance. In a recent *Harvard Business Review* article, Deloitte policy states the following:

> Our design calls for every team leader to check in with each team member once a week. For us, these check-ins are not in addition to the work of a team leader; they are the work of a team leader. If a leader checks in less often than once a week, the team member's priorities may become vague and aspirational, and the leader can't be as helpful—and the conversation will shift from coaching for near-term work to giving feedback about past performance.[4]

In your church or organization, you might not need a weekly check-in. The optimum frequency might be monthly, but I would suggest having at least a quarterly conversation. The monthly or quarterly check-ins keep issues from piling up and engage you in an ongoing conversation rather than a one-time-a-year evaluation. If you are having honest, frequent conversations, the annual review shouldn't include any surprises.

If your organization still decides to do a more formal annual review, I encourage you to think of it as an annual summary. Because all year long through your regular, more informal conversations you have been evaluating, assessing, and adjusting. Therefore, the annual review (summary) is nothing more than compiling into one report what you have been talking about all year.

Also, make the meeting a conversation, not a monologue. This meeting doesn't need to feel like a top-down download from supervisor to employee. Include the person you are managing in the discussion. I have often walked into a meeting with a staff member I was leading, thinking I had all the facts and a clear picture of what was going on. However, I discovered I had only a partial view of reality. And to get a complete view, I needed to invite their perspective.

Good leaders will see these conversations as opportunities for them to discover how they can better help the person on their team succeed. One of your primary jobs in managing people is to remove barriers that keep them from accomplishing their priorities. These monthly or quarterly conversations are great times to talk about those barriers. But as a supervisor, that requires you to listen, not just talk.

These conversations are the time not only to listen and dialogue but also to bring up any area where the person on your team is underperforming. In these meetings, you want to be relational and conversational. You want to invite the person's perspective. But you also must courageously wear your supervisor hat. You must be clear and, if necessary, willing to have the uncomfortable conversation and confront underperformance.

If you manage other people, I want to offer you a challenge. When it comes to people not performing well, keep short accounts with those you lead. Don't let underperformance pile up. When you begin to notice that someone isn't performing up to expectations, address the issue in the next monthly or quarterly conversation. Doing so feels more like real-time coaching rather than an annual report card. However, when you stockpile a person's underperformance and then at their annual review unload on them things that happened months ago, you devalue and deflate them.

To get more tactical, I suggest keeping the monthly or quarterly conversation to about a half hour. Don't make this a regular meeting to discuss ongoing projects. This meeting is intended to discuss their overall performance.

Here are a few questions you might consider thinking through or asking in this monthly or quarterly conversation:

- Is the person you manage clear about their job description, priorities, and goals? If any of their responsibilities have changed, this might be a good time to pull out their job description and consider making an adjustment. But even more important than the person being clear about their job description, it is imperative that they be clear about their priorities. "The research clearly shows that one of the most important determinants of the effectiveness of the performance management system is the goal setting process."[5]
- What's going well? Where do they feel like they are winning?
- Where do they feel stuck?

- Where are they experiencing frustration in their job?
- Where do they need to improve?

This is the moment as the supervisor that you need to be honest and clear. As much as possible, give them tangible steps they can take.

- How can you as the supervisor better help this person succeed?
- What action steps have you each agreed to take as a result of this meeting?

I suggest writing down the action steps and sending a copy to the team member. Then you can review them together during your next performance conversation.

I know this topic can feel very organizational. But I want to conclude by reminding you of the "why" behind performance evaluation. It is about the following motivations:

- *Stewarding your purpose.* Your ministry has a high and holy calling. You have been given a purpose with eternal impact. But you have been given limited resources—and you will be accountable for those resources. The most significant resources you have been given are the staff or volunteers who serve on your team. Your teams should work hard and have clear priorities. Their performance matters. Because of your mission and eternal purpose, you must be willing to have the uncomfortable performance conversations.
- *Valuing your people.* You engage in performance evaluation not only because your purpose matters. You also do it because your people matter. You want to treat them with dignity and respect and to honor them as mature adults. As a general rule, I believe the people on your team want to do their job well. And I believe most of them really do want honest feedback and coaching.

Perhaps you and your organization need to rethink how you assess performance. Maybe it's time to jettison the old wineskin that feels like an IRS audit and craft a process that is personal, conversational, and helpful.

TEAM DISCUSSION QUESTIONS

1. What is good about your current performance review process?
2. What could be better?
3. What components does a good performance review have?
4. When you are the one receiving a performance review, what can you do to make it a beneficial experience?

14

How to Raise Your Team's Productivity by 30 Percent

It has been said that if you want to kill time, a meeting is the perfect weapon. We've all been there. You are sitting in a meeting, coming to the end of the allotted time. You start to get restless. You begin shutting down your computer and putting your stuff in your backpack. You discreetly glance at your phone and see a couple of text messages that have come in. Your mind has already shifted to the rest of your day.

The meeting ends and everyone quickly exits. And no one has the time to stop and ask, "Was that a good meeting?" "Did we really accomplish what we needed to?" "Was it an effective and productive use of our time?" Sometimes after a meeting that was a complete waste of time, I have cynically figured out how much salary and how many staff hours we just squandered.

Apparently we have good reason to feel frustrated by ineffective meetings:

- Professionals lose 31 hours per month in unproductive meetings (roughly four work days).
- Approximately 11 million meetings occur in the US each and every day.
- Most professionals attend a total of 61.8 meetings per month.

- Research indicates that over 50 percent of this meeting time is wasted.
- In one study, 73 percent of people said they have brought other work to meetings, and 39 percent say they have dozed during meetings.[1]

Here is what I know to be true:

- Your organization spends a lot of valuable time and resources on meetings.
- Your team wants to be helpful and productive.
- It is discouraging and frustrating to walk away from a meeting feeling like it was a waste of time.
- With just a few small tweaks, you can better steward people's time, your organization's resources, and the effectiveness of your impact.

After sitting in thousands of meetings, I have concluded that the most important part of any meeting is the "landing." And yet it is usually the most neglected part of the meeting. The norm is to walk out of a meeting without clear decisions, action steps, and deliverables.

Just as I have sat in thousands of meetings, I have also been on thousands of flights. But I have never been on a flight where the pilot neglected the landing. Every pilot knows it doesn't matter how good the snacks were or how good the in-flight movie was or how clean the bathrooms were; if you don't land well, the flight was a disaster. By the way, the pilot's job is to land the plane. It's not the passengers' responsibility. In the same way, if you are leading a meeting, you need to assume the role of pilot. Your job is to make sure you land the meeting well and get clear decisions and action steps.

As far as meetings go, it doesn't matter how clear the agenda was or how good the snacks were or how much good discussion took place. If you don't land the meeting well, it can be an organizational disaster. I have developed a strategy to help the meetings I lead land well. A crash landing isn't good for a plane—and it isn't good for a meeting. A good landing of a plane is gradual and takes time. Landing a meeting well also takes time. Most meetings continue discussion up to the very last minute, and then they take a crash landing. I have found it to be good practice to reserve the last fifteen minutes of a meeting to land well. Setting aside the last fifteen minutes allows for a smooth, effective, and productive landing.

I have also learned that asking and answering three questions during that fifteen minutes can significantly raise the productivity of the meeting.

Question 1: What did we decide?

I am amazed by how many times I have walked out of a meeting thinking we made a decision on something, only to learn later that other people who had sat in the same meeting did not think we had landed on a decision. Unfortunately, I started to act on the decisions I *thought* we had made. This caused significant confusion, chaos, and conflict. By the way, such a situation can make you pretty unpopular with your teammates. Before you leave the meeting, you must be clear on what is a decision and what is still a discussion.

To use a football analogy, it's the difference between standing in a huddle and running a play. When you are standing in the huddle, you are just discussing options and possibilities. Running a play means a decision has been made and you are now free to move into action. One moment signals the transition from a huddle to a play. That moment is when the center snaps the ball. At that instant everyone moves into action.

Imagine the team standing around in the huddle, when the tight end breaks from the huddle, grabs the ball, and starts running down the field. It would certainly not be an effective or productive play. In football, everybody in the huddle must be absolutely clear about what play was called. And nobody starts executing the play until the ball is snapped. I have been in (and led) many staff meetings where it wasn't clear if the ball had been snapped (a clear decision had been made).

Now, when I lead meetings, I find myself always pushing for decisions. I have been in meetings, just like you have, where we are so close to making a decision but nothing is ever definitively decided. I have also been in meetings where we end up rehashing everything we discussed in the last meeting. It's like the movie *Groundhog Day*—and it's a waste of time.

And because we have an amazing ability to interpret things differently, I have found it helpful to actually write down on a whiteboard or flip chart the decisions that were made in a meeting.

Question 2: Who needs to know what we decided?

I have had personal discussions with hundreds of church staff members about the issue of "staff culture." When talking about gaps or weaknesses, lack of communication comes up in almost every discussion. This has direct correlation to the question "What did we decide?" If decisions aren't clear, then there is no way communication will be clear or accurate.

Communication is also another reason I have found it helpful to write down the decisions made in team meetings. When decisions are written down, team leaders are able to take what is written back to their teams. It also minimizes the chances of decisions being reinterpreted between the team meeting and the time a decision gets communicated.

Playwright George Bernard Shaw is attributed as saying, "The single biggest problem in communication is the illusion that it has taken place." In most churches I have worked with, the leadership would give themselves higher scores for communication than the volunteers or staff that worked in the organization would give them.

The question "Who needs to know what we decided?" forces me to think about the issue of communication. Most of the time, after I have left a meeting, I have quickly moved on to the next meeting or task. I didn't take the time to think about my team members and how the decisions made in the meeting might impact them.

People love to be "in the know," and people especially love to be in the know when decisions are made that impact them. Communication not only shares information; it also makes people feel valued. But the flip side of that statement is also true. One way we make people feel devalued is to under-communicate. As part of that last fifteen minutes in a meeting, think through the communication that is needed based on the decisions just made.

As Patrick Lencioni talks about, we must learn the practice and discipline of cascading communication down through the organization.[2] And as a leader, one of my assignments from the meeting is to communicate those decisions to those I work with. A few minutes of communication on the front end of a decision will help your team be more effective, make your team members feel valued, and save a lot of time because you won't have to clean up a big mess later due to lack of communication.

Question 3: Who is responsible and what are the action steps? Key deliverables?

As important as it is to have clear decisions and clear communication, it is just as important to know who is responsible for certain actions. Ultimately, all ideas and decisions become work that somebody has to own.

To go back to the football analogy, it is deciding which part of the play each person is responsible for. Sometimes the responsibility will be obvious because of people's roles, but sometimes it is less obvious, and in those times clarity is key. After writing down the decision the team makes, I suggest also writing down any key action items related to that decision and who is responsible for them. I would also include the date the person will commit to having the action item completed.

I know this process might seem a bit tedious, but these steps can be what move good discussion and good intentions to great progress and great effectiveness. If you are a smaller team, these steps might seem like overkill. I encourage you to still employ the concepts but customize them to your size and situation.

Think of your meeting as raw electricity. It is full of life and energy and potential and endless possibilities. But raw electricity can also be dangerous and harmful. For that electricity to be useful and productive, it needs to be harnessed and directed. It needs a transformer. The last fifteen minutes of your meeting are the transformer that takes the raw electricity of great ideas and discussion and directs it so that it can now be productive for your organization.

You can also take two more small steps to increase the productivity of your team meetings.

Just as landing a plane is significant, so is takeoff. One strategy I employ to help a meeting take off well is to ask the following question right at the beginning: "What is the win (or purpose) for this meeting?" By asking that question, we align everyone's expectations and define what success is for the meeting. It is amazing how many times that question is met with blank stares. Another way to ask it is, "What outcomes would make this meeting worth the investment of our time?"

The final small tweak to make meetings more productive happens in the ten minutes after the meeting. Whenever a pilot parks a plane at the Jetway, they don't immediately exit the plane. No! They have paperwork to fill out. The flight isn't over just because the plane has landed. The same is true with meetings. Just like a pilot, after you have landed a meeting, it is helpful to take some time to jot down important notes.

After the meeting is over, if you are the team leader, I encourage you to reserve ten minutes before your next task or meeting. And then take that ten minutes to capture what was decided in the meeting, communication that needs to happen, and who is responsible for key action items. Also write down anything you need to follow up on before the next meeting.

Finally, take those notes and place them as item 1 on the agenda for the next meeting with that team. Reviewing decisions, communication, and deliverables will help raise the level of accountability for all of those involved.

Meetings are part of life in any organization and an aspect of the process of moving the vision forward. High-performing teams learn how to maximize and optimize the time spent in meetings.

TEAM DISCUSSION QUESTIONS

1. As a general rule, how do you think your team does at having productive and effective meetings? What could you do to improve your team meetings?
2. Is there a meeting you could eliminate or at least shorten?
3. What are the characteristics of a well-led meeting?
4. What are the characteristics of a poorly led meeting?

PART 4

GET 'ER DONE

A lot of brilliant ideas, strategies, and innovation fail abysmally, not because of lack of clarity, but because of a lack of execution. The execution of priorities is where the rubber meets the road for high-performing teams. In this section, we will help your team improve productivity and tenacious execution.

15

~~Work~~ Stewardship Ethic

The 2008 men's US Olympic basketball team was perhaps the best-ever group of players to all wear the same uniform. There is a well-known story that Dwayne Wade and Chris Bosh tell about the training camp for these celebrity athletes.

"We're in Las Vegas and we all come down for team breakfast at the start of the whole training camp," Bosh said. "And Kobe comes in with ice on his knees and with his trainers. He's got sweat drenched through his workout gear. And I'm like, 'It's 8 o'clock in the morning, man. Where is he coming from?'"

Wade added, "Everybody else just woke up. . . . We're all yawning, and he's already three hours and a full workout into his day."[1]

One of the highest compliments ever paid Kobe Bryant was by his basketball idol Michael Jordan. Jordan said Kobe was the only player to ever approach his own work ethic. Even in high school, Kobe would show up at the gym at 5:00 a.m. and practice until 7:00 a.m. before going to class.

As an NBA star, he was always the first one to the gym, even when he was hurt. During practice he would count all his successful shots and wouldn't quit practice until he made four hundred shots. During games he would watch film of himself at halftime to see how he could improve in the second half.

In 2008, he even had Nike shave a few millimeters off the bottom of his shoes to get a hundredth of a second better reaction time.[2]

Having a strong work ethic is right. It is morally noble. It makes us better people and benefits our ministries. But for us as Christ-followers, there is a deeper issue than working hard because it is right. And that is the issue of stewardship. Rather than talking about a strong work ethic, I prefer to talk about a strong stewardship ethic. We are not owners; we are stewards. And as a steward, I am accountable for that which has been entrusted to me. I am a steward of my gifts, my finances, my relationships, my time . . . and yes, my ministry assignment. My highest accountability is not to my supervisor but to the Lord who has entrusted me with my job.

As I read about Kobe Bryant's work ethic, I was struck by the internal drive that kept pushing him year after year. But I was most impressed by all the microsteps he took to constantly improve his game and make him one of the best to ever play professional basketball.

Little steps can make a big difference. Proactive steps can take your ministry game to a whole new level. In the same way, little compromises and minor lapses in discipline can lead to failure.

> I walked by the field of a lazy person,
>> the vineyard of one with no common sense.
> I saw that it was overgrown with nettles.
>> It was covered with weeds,
>> and its walls were broken down.
> Then, as I looked and thought about it,
>> I learned this lesson:
> A little extra sleep, a little more slumber,
>> a little folding of the hands to rest—
> then poverty will pounce on you like a bandit;
>> scarcity will attack you like an armed robber. (Prov. 24:30–34 NLT)

Solomon shows us the disastrous results of a poor work ethic. The scene he describes in verses 30 and 31 didn't come about because of a major natural disaster. A tornado didn't blow through town nor did a group of thugs vandalize the vineyard. The garden's condition was the result of daily neglect. The word that most stands out to me in the passage is *little*. It is used three times in verse 33. Just a *little* more sleep.

Just a *little* more time to chill out and relax. Little decisions can lead to big problems.

Diligent Dozen

In the spirit of Proverbs 24, I want to talk about my "Diligent Dozen" when it comes to a strong stewardship ethic. These are twelve practices that evidence a strong work ethic. When you live these out, you win, your team wins, your ministry wins, and the kingdom wins.

1. Show up on time.

Punctuality is not so much about being on time as it is respecting other people's time and your own commitments. The small decision to always be punctual is evidence of a good work ethic.

I remember once being invited to a meeting with about a dozen other people. The person leading the meeting sent word that he was going to be late. He showed up an hour and a half late. There was no emergency. He just had some other "important" things he had to take care of. It was frustrating, and I remember feeling very disrespected. His tardiness wasted eighteen hours of time for the people who showed up for that meeting.

I have found that for me to be punctual, I have to do a good job of managing my schedule. One of the best rules is to always put a little buffer between meetings and appointments. As you well know, meetings don't always end on time and there are moments (especially in ministry) when you can't shut down a conversation and say, "I'm sorry, but our time is up." For years my days were scheduled with back-to-back meetings and appointments. I always felt hurried, rushing from one thing to the next. Scheduling five or ten minutes between meetings allows for a little breathing room—and even a bathroom break!

2. Do it now (don't procrastinate).

I love this quote from one of the characters in the movie *Despicable Me*: "I'm doing things I don't need to do in order to avoid doing anything I'm actually supposed to do."[3] Or maybe you can relate to the guy who said, "I'm a multitasking procrastinator. I can put off multiple things at once."

Do you sometimes have tasks or projects that sit on your to-do list for weeks? Three actions have helped me deal with procrastination in my own life:

- *Give yourself a deadline.* Even if it is a self-imposed artificial deadline, it can still help you feel a sense of urgency.
- *Do hard things first.* Most of us like to check stuff off our to-do list and so we often start with those things that are easiest to get done. By the time we get to the big stuff, we are out of steam or have squandered the most productive part of our day.
- *Break it down.* Sometimes the size of a project can be overwhelming and paralyzing. But breaking down the project into small, doable tasks makes the work more manageable.

And remember, there are seven days in a week and someday isn't one of them.

3. Take initiative.

This is about being a self-starter. Every supervisor loves to have people on their team who are proactive and self-initiating. They are not passive, sitting around waiting to be told what to do.

Being a self-starter is not about gifting, it is about a mind-set. It is about choosing to have an internal attitude that is proactive.

4. Care about the whole.

People who have a strong work ethic don't just care about their area or department. They don't view their area as an independent silo, but rather they are clear about how their area contributes to the organization's mission and vision. And when needed, they are more than willing to lend a hand to help another team succeed. In a healthy culture, you think more like basketball players than golfers. In golf, your individual score matters. In basketball, the only score that matters is the collective score. You win or lose as a team.

5. Beware of little foxes.

In Song of Solomon, Solomon talks about "the little foxes that ruin the vineyard." Once again, notice the word *little*. Constant little distractions will chip away at our work ethic.

Some studies of office workers have revealed that they constantly stop what they're doing to read and respond to incoming emails. It is not unusual for them to glance at their in-box thirty to forty times an hour.

What is it that is most likely to distract you from your work?

6. Raise your hand (do more than is required).

Be hungry to help. Take on assignments that nobody else wants to do. It is a huge compliment to be known in the organization as the go-to or get-'er-done person.

"The appetite of laborers works for them; their hunger drives them on" (Prov. 16:26). Solomon is talking about physical hunger being the motivation that drives the worker. But what I am talking about is the hunger to contribute, the hunger to see the vision move forward.

7. Follow through.

When you say you will do something, you do it. Your yes is yes and your no is no. You are dependable and reliable. Your boss doesn't have to check up on you to make sure something got done.

Carl Jung is quoted as saying, "You are what you do, not what you say you'll do."

Doing a good job with follow-through means paying attention to details. You don't do sloppy work. For example, when you send emails, they are thought through, well written, and free of errors. When it comes to work ethic, not only the quantity of effort matters, so does the quality of effort. You don't get points for working hard while being careless or incompetent.

Excellence in your work will increase your influence in the ministry.

8. Don't make excuses.

People with a strong work ethic take full responsibility. They practice extreme ownership.

"Implementing Extreme Ownership requires checking your ego and operating with a high degree of humility. Admitting mistakes, taking ownership, and developing a plan to overcome challenges are integral to any successful team."[4]

People with a compelling work ethic don't make excuses. Solomon says that one of the things that characterizes a slacker is that they make baseless excuses.

> The lazy person claims, "There's a lion out there!
> If I go outside, I might be killed!" (Prov. 22:13 NLT)

9. Over-deliver.

I like the old saying "under-promise and over-deliver." Don't just do the minimum required. Don't do just enough to get by.

I love going into a restaurant where the service and the environment and the food all exceed my expectations.

10. Have a can-do spirit.

Learn to lead with yes. When new ideas and changes are introduced, instead of giving the five reasons the suggestion might not work, have a positive, eager attitude. Learn phrases such as "We can do this," "We will figure it out," and "We can make it happen."

11. Leave everything better than you found it.

One day I was having lunch with Chip Ingram, a well-known pastor and radio Bible teacher. After the meal we both went to the men's restroom. We were standing next to each other at the sink. I washed my hands and walked toward the door. As I glanced back, Chip had grabbed a couple of extra paper towels. Splashes of water and soap were all over the countertop. Chip was cleaning them up.

On the way out of the restaurant that day, he told me that early in his faith journey he had been challenged to always leave everything better than he found it.

What a great principle to live by.

12. Be faithful.

Faithfulness isn't concerned about the size of the job. Faithfulness doesn't fret about the importance of the job. Faithfulness doesn't worry about who gets credit for the job. The proving ground for tomorrow's opportunities is today's faithfulness. And there are no shortcuts. The path to greater kingdom influence runs through anonymous faithfulness.

> If you are faithful in little things, you will be faithful in large ones. But if you are dishonest in little things, you won't be honest with greater responsibilities. (Luke 16:10 NLT)

Make it your goal to just be faithful and leave it to God what doors He opens and what platform He gives you. Joseph in the book of Genesis is a great example of someone who was faithful in every circumstance and every job, and God eventually elevated him to be the second most powerful man in all of Egypt.

My challenge for you each day is to show up—palms up. Palms up is the idea of openness and willingness to do whatever is needed, whether or not it is in your job description. Keep your head down and let God raise you up.

Let me ask you to take a courageous step with this chapter's content. Ask your supervisor what you could do to have a stronger work ethic. Have them look over the Diligent Dozen and identify one or two of these practices they think you could improve on.

And let Ephesians 6:7 be your guiding motivation.

> Work with enthusiasm, as though you were working for the Lord rather than for people. (NLT)

TEAM DISCUSSION QUESTIONS

1. Read back over Proverbs 24:30–34. What most stands out to you? Why?

2. How important is punctuality to you? How significant of a value is it in your team?

3. In your role, what are some practical ways you can implement the principle of "Leave it better than you found it"?

4. Which of the Diligent Dozen could you do better? Is there one of the Diligent Dozen that your team should focus on?

16

"Nailed It!"

Teddy Roosevelt gave the following famous speech in Paris in 1910:

It is not the critic who counts; not the man who points out how the strong man stumbles, or where the doer of deeds could have done them better. The credit belongs to the man who is actually in the arena, whose face is marred by dust and sweat and blood; who strives valiantly; who errs, who comes short again and again, because there is no effort without error and shortcoming; but who does actually strive to do the deeds; who knows great enthusiasms, the great devotions; who spends himself in a worthy cause; who at the best knows in the end the triumph of high achievement, and who at the worst, if he fails, at least fails while daring greatly, so that his place shall never be with those cold and timid souls who neither know victory nor defeat.[1]

The words that jump off the page at me are *who does actually strive to do the deeds*. Roosevelt said that credit doesn't go to the critic or the philosopher or the politician or the communicator but rather to the one who executes. He praised the person who actually strives to do the deeds—who delivers, implements, and executes.

Every organization and ministry has "go-to" people. In other words, when senior leaders want something to get done, they know whom they can count on to step up and deliver.

If you have been in ministry more than a week, you have discovered that all vision eventually comes down to hard work. It doesn't take long for the inspiration of vision to morph into the perspiration of effort. Execution of priorities is where the rubber meets the road of high-performing teams.

"Unless you translate big thoughts into concrete steps for action, they're pointless. Without execution, the breakthrough thinking breaks down, learning adds no value, people don't meet their stretch goals, and the revolution stops dead in its tracks."[2]

A lot of brilliant ideas, strategies, and innovation fail abysmally because of a lack of execution. In earlier chapters, we talked about the critical importance of identifying and establishing priorities. Prioritizing is what we do ahead of time. It requires thinking, discernment, and space. Execution is what we do now that we are clear about our priorities. This requires diligence, discipline, and focus.

So often what keeps our ministries stuck isn't a poorly designed website or an outdated logo or lack of clarity about our mission. It's the inability to execute. Execution fills the gap between plans and results, between wishful thinking and actual progress.

Sometimes those of us who wear the label of "leader" or have the spiritual gift of leadership may think we can skip this chapter. After all, execution is about the tactics, the details, the micro. Execution doesn't sound sexy, and it's the stuff leaders like to delegate. However, while leaders should be expectant about the future, they better be helping their teams execute in the present.

The authors of the book *Execution* are spot-on when they say, "Leadership without the discipline of execution is incomplete and ineffective. Without the ability to execute, all other attributes of leadership become hollow."[3]

If you are a team leader, a supervisor, or a senior leader, this chapter is for you also.

When I think about the work of ministry teams, it breaks down into the following four components.

VISION ➤ STRATEGY ➤ PRIORITIES ➤ EXECUTION

Here is how this might look in a church:

Vision . . . to transform their region.

Strategy . . . launching campuses around the region.

Priorities . . . locations and leaders (leadership pipeline).

Execution . . . carrying out the thousands of actions required to develop leaders, secure new locations, and launch healthy campuses.

As a leader, while you can't know every detail, your responsibility is to make sure the people and teams in your ministry are executing. And maybe more importantly, your responsibility is to remove the organizational impediments that keep them from executing effectively.

Let me share some strategies that will be helpful for you personally and for your teams when it comes to executing priorities.

Eliminate the Nonessential

Chinese author and philosopher Lin Yutang said, "Besides the noble art of getting things done, there is the noble art of leaving things undone. The wisdom of life consists of the elimination of nonessentials."[4]

As Anne Lamott says, "No is a complete sentence."[5]

This principle is built on the fundamental belief that the greatest results come by narrowing our focus. One reason some of us feel like we are spinning our wheels in our ministries is because we are trying to do too much. As a result, we feel scattered and behind.

Did you know that in the two years after Steve Jobs returned to Apple in 1997, he took the company from 350 products to 10? That's 340 nos.[6]

I do a lot of personal coaching of leaders, and I like to have them do an exercise when we come to the first of the year. I call it "Trim the Fat." I ask them to do a bit of a time audit. And then I ask them this question: "If I forced you to eliminate 20 percent of what you are spending time on, what would you cut?" In other words, of all that you give your time to, what is the least fruitful 20 percent? I would ask you the same question—what are you spending time on that is a low return on investment?

Add 50 Percent

Human beings have an amazing ability to underestimate. For example, when my wife and I go to the grocery store together, just before we put our items on the checkout stand, we both make a guess as to what our basket full of groceries will cost. Even though I have done this hundreds of times, at least 95 percent of the time I still guess low.

We do the same thing when it comes to assessing how long it will take to execute a task or project. Think of remodeling a house. Have you ever once heard someone say their remodel took less time and cost less than they originally thought?

In one study, thirty-seven students were asked how long they thought it would take them to complete their senior thesis. When the students were asked how long it would take "if everything went as well as it possibly could," their averaged estimate was 27.4 days. When they were asked how long it would take "if everything went as poorly as it possibly could," their averaged estimate was 48.6 days. In the end, the average time it took the students was 55.5 days.[7]

By the way, studies show our propensity to underestimate also applies to tasks we have done before. In his excellent book *Essentialism*, Greg McKeown writes, "One way to protect against this is simply to add a 50% buffer to the amount of time we estimate it will take to complete a task or project."[8]

Attack One Thing at a Time

An enormous amount of research has conclusively demonstrated that multitasking is ineffective. "People don't multitask because they're good at it. They do it because they are more distracted. They have trouble inhibiting the impulse to do another activity."[9]

Remember that all tasks and projects are not equal in priority. This is not about starting at the top of your to-do list and working your way down. First, you must have clarity on what is most important so you can attack the right thing. Get in the habit of constantly asking, "What is it today or this week that by executing on it will yield the most fruit for the ministry?"

Next, you must remove the distractions that seduce and tempt you. For instance, if I am going to focus on writing, I need to either have my phone in another room or at least turn it facedown on the desk. What is it in your world that constantly calls your name and gets you off task? Seriously, what is it? And what step can you take to mitigate that distraction?

Learn How to Sprint

If you read books on personal productivity or organizational effectiveness, you will hear people talk about "sprints."

The most literal understanding of a sprint is when a runner exerts maximum effort that results in a burst of speed. And they run as fast as they can for a short distance. That becomes a great metaphor for how to execute most effectively. A sprint is a fairly short, concentrated period of time when we accelerate our progress.

This has become a fairly common term to describe how individuals and teams can be the most effective. When dealing with an individual, it might be that you set aside a one-hour sprint for them to work on a project. The idea is to have one full hour of undistracted, focused effort on the task at hand. When people are sprinting, they don't multitask. All their effort is laser focused on one objective.

In a ministry or organization, you might have your team do a one-week sprint. During that time the team discusses and comes to agreement on what will be accomplished in the coming week. There is clarity and agreement around priorities and expectations. There is also focus on executing on those priorities. And lastly, there is kind but firm accountability for accomplishing the desired results.

Don't Just Expect—Inspect

The book *4 Disciplines of Execution* contains an astounding statistic. "We have asked hundreds of thousands of employees in various industries around the globe to respond to the statement: 'I meet at least monthly with my manager to discuss my progress on goals.' To our surprise, only

34 percent can respond positively to this statement, even when the review is only once each month."[10]

My suspicion is that in ministry organizations that number would be even lower.

A few years ago I was trained in a process called StratOp, a strategic planning process developed by Tom Paterson. A company called OtterBox was our case study and a big aha for me was seeing how they turned a strategic planning tool into an execution accountability tool. Every three weeks or so, each department director at OtterBox met with the executive team for something like fifteen minutes. And in that fifteen minutes, they reviewed their key priorities. Each existing priority was given a color—red, yellow, or green—to indicate their current status. Green meant it was flourishing. Yellow meant there were some concerns. Red meant it was tanking and needed serious attention. One thing I love about the colors is that it is a visual report card.

The brief meeting was also a time when new priorities were established. One of the department directors for OtterBox was in our training, and she told me, "Obviously, not everything I do is talked about in that brief meeting with senior leadership, but that fifteen minutes gives me a sense of how my team is doing, clarifies what is most important, and identifies exactly what I am going to be graded on." I love that! Clarity is a beautiful thing. And that kind of clarity gives focused direction to execution.

OtterBox's approach certainly isn't the only accountability tool. Another tool you might consider implementing is something Bill Hybels developed so he could be more focused and effective. It is his 6 × 6 card. It identifies the 6 key priorities he is focused on in the next 6 weeks. There is nothing magical about having 6 priorities or working on them over 6 weeks. The magic is in the clarity of focus. For you it might be 4 × 4. But find a tool that helps you and those you manage to have laser focus on what is most important.[11]

Remember, there is no vision without execution! And in the words of Teddy Roosevelt, credit goes to the one "who does actually strive to do the deeds."

TEAM DISCUSSION QUESTIONS

1. If I forced you to eliminate 20 percent of what you spend time on, what would you eliminate?

2. If you were to grade yourself for your execution over the last two weeks, what grade would you give? Why?

3. What would help your team take its execution to an even higher level?

4. How often is your work inspected by someone in authority over you? If you are a supervisor, how effectively are you inspecting the work of those you oversee?

17

Just Do It

O
ther people's worship becomes our stewardship." That is a quote
from my friend James Duvall, who as a pastor has become a bit of
a productivity guru. What James means by that statement is that other
people's acts of worship through giving are what fund our ministries—
and for some of us, our salaries. They have entrusted their money to our
ministries and now their acts of worship become our acts of stewardship.
And that doesn't just mean handling the budget responsibly. It also means
we steward our assignment responsibly by working hard and being fruitful.

It reminds me of the parable of the talents (see Matt. 25:14–30). Each
of the three men in the story was given a divine assignment. They had each
been entrusted with a differing amount of talents. Verse 19 says that after
a long time, the master returned to settle the accounts with his servants.
The first two servants had been productive and fruitful and received the
praise of the master.

However, the third servant had done nothing with what he had been given.
The master didn't tell him to try a little harder next time. He didn't say
the servant was ineffective. Nor did he simply conclude the servant hadn't
reached his full potential. No! Some of the harshest words Jesus would ever
utter were directed toward this servant who squandered his divine assignment. The servant was neither fruitful nor productive with what he had

been given. In verse 26, when addressing the servant, the master calls him a wicked, lazy servant. And in verse 30, he commands that this "useless" servant be thrown "into outer darkness." *Wow!* Jesus didn't mince any words about His expectation that we be fruitful with what we've been given.

So, in this chapter, I want to talk about how we can raise our level of productivity and fruitfulness.

Top Five Best Practices for Productivity

I believe the first aspect of being productive has to do with mental attitude. Before we ever talk about techniques, tips, and time management strategies, we have to talk about the heart. What we do in ministry matters—for eternity. We are not just making widgets (and there's nothing wrong with making widgets), but the stakes are much higher in what we are called to do. I hope your drive to be fruitful doesn't come from an unhealthy place of people pleasing or trying to find your worth in what you accomplish. I hope your desire to be fruitful comes from a deep love for God and a sobering sense of stewardship.

Now, let me give you my top five best practices for being productive.

1. Take outlandish control of your schedule.

"People do not decide their futures, they decide their habits and their habits decide their futures."[1]

I love that statement. I get to decide the habits I will have at work that decide how fruitful I will be.

You might be tempted to pin your lack of productivity on the fact that you're not in charge. It's the organizational environment that's the problem. It's the constant change. It's the lack of communication. It's the absence of clear direction. It's the organizational politics. I get it! I know those issues can be factors, but we have far more control than we want to admit.

You must be proactive, diligent, and protective when it comes to owning your work hours. Everybody has a plan for your life and how you should spend your time. Especially with technology today, you are constantly being invited, lured, cajoled, and enticed to spend time on things that aren't productive.

"We would never leave our wallet out and think it's ok for people to come and take whatever money they want or need."[2]

You have to think about your minutes and hours and weeks in the same way. You can't let random requests, social media, trivial interruptions, hallway conversations, or meaningless tasks steal your time.

One of the most helpful practices I have implemented is trying to never say yes in the moment. Saying yes in the moment has caused more frustration in my ministry and marriage than almost anything else.

The problem with saying yes in the moment is that you rarely have a clear and good picture of all that you are saying yes to. My friend Doug Slaybaugh, who hired me at Saddleback, regularly says, "Just remember, there is no innocent yes." This is the principle of the distant elephant. Off in the distance, even a giant elephant looks small. But once it gets closer, its size becomes overwhelming. Stepping back before you agree to something allows you to take an honest look at all that is involved as well as its impact on your current pace and load.

2. Calendarize your priorities.

Did you know that only 41 percent of tasks on a to-do list ever get done?

Highly productive people put everything on their calendar, and then work and live by that calendar.[3]

This is critical. Your priorities have to become calendar appointments.

Your calendar is where your priorities and your time converge.

Here is an equation for being productive:

Clarity + Courage + Calendar = Productivity

The order is important.

Clarity—What are the "must do's" in your job? What is mission critical for you to accomplish?

Courage—Will you have the guts to execute on the things that are most important? Will you say no to the good so you can give yourself to the best? It takes courage to eliminate the nonessential.

Calendar—This is where your values and priorities get operationalized.

Your calendar is far more than a way to keep you organized and get you to meetings on time. It is a primary tool for helping you become who you want to become.

Learn to live life and do ministry from your calendar, not a to-do list. If you really need to get something done, give it dedicated space on your schedule.

To do this well, you need to get out ahead of your current obligations and block off the necessary time for focusing on your priorities. You might need to look ahead a month or more so you can block time on your calendar for your most important work.

I love what Kevin Kruse says about this: "Treat your time blocked work as if they were appointments with your doctor."[4]

There is something about deciding when you are going to do something that significantly increases the likelihood of your actually doing it.

In the book *The Power of Full Engagement*, the authors describe a study in which a group of women agreed to do a breast self-exam. One group was told to simply do it in the next thirty days. The other group was asked to decide when and where in the next thirty days they were going to do it. Only 53 percent of the first group did the self-exam. But 100 percent of the women who said when and where they would do the exam completed it.[5]

3. Focus on minutes, not hours.

Several years ago, my wife's uncle served as an admiral in the navy. At the time it was his job to purchase aircrafts for the navy, and he worked out of the Pentagon. When we were in Washington, DC, he invited us to have lunch with him at the Pentagon. As I walked around with him, I was amazed by how many people saluted me. Okay, it's possible they might have been saluting him. But I noticed that he had a little card in his hand that he kept referring to. Later he told me that it was his daily schedule. When he arrived at the Pentagon, each day his assistant would hand him a card that listed all his appointments for the day, including the time and location.

What was amazing to me was that his day was broken down into fifteen-minute increments. Every single day was meticulously orchestrated in order for him to achieve maximum productivity.

Now, most of us probably don't require a schedule that is broken down into fifteen-minute increments, but if we want to become more productive, we need to think in minutes, not just hours.

You must master your minutes to master your life.[6]

High-performing people "focus on minutes, not hours. Most people default to hour and half-hour blocks on their calendar; highly successful people know that there are 1,440 minutes in every day and that there is nothing more valuable than time."[7]

I was teaching on the topic of productivity to a staff team recently and was talking about this issue of seeing your day in minutes, not just half-hour or hour-long chunks of time. The senior pastor had an aha moment. He said, "Whenever someone tries to get with me, my default is to give them a one-on-one meeting for an hour. I need to stop assuming that everyone needs an hour. I suspect there are a lot of my meetings that could be handled in fifteen or twenty minutes."

4. Take notice, stay curious, and write everything down.

I hate when I'm at a restaurant and my waiter walks up to take my order and doesn't write anything down. Inevitably something gets a little messed up with the order.

I remember an experience I had several years ago that was very frustrating. One of the young girls that was in my first church grew up and got married. She married a young man who was in seminary and felt called to ministry. They were going to be in Southern California for a video game convention (that should have been my first clue that things might not go well). They asked if Connie and I would have dinner with them, so we drove up to meet them for the evening. We spent almost two hours with them—and this young aspiring pastor never asked one ministry question, nor did he write anything down. I walked away thinking, *I'm way more curious at forty-five than this kid is at twenty-five.* I want to stay curious my whole life. I want to constantly keep getting better. And I want to capture the best thinking of those around me. One way to do that is to write stuff down, type notes into your iPad, or record a conversation.

Richard Branson, the founder of the Virgin Group, offered one piece of advice for 2017 for his employees.

Have an idea? Write it down. Hear an interesting point from a friend? See or hear an interesting article, documentary, podcast, book or film? Write it down. Wake up in the middle of the night remembering a dream? Write it down. Anything at all happen? Write it down. Ever since I was a child I have made lists of all kinds, including short-term tasks, long-term goals and resolutions. It's how I make sense of the world, bring order to the ideas in my head, and start turning them into action. In 2017, get yourself a notebook, or an iPad app, or a pen to write on your hand. However you do it, take note: if you don't take notes, your ideas will get lost.[8]

Who is the most productive person you know? Why not sit down and interview them. What habits and practices do they have that you can learn from?

Be observant. Take notice of healthy and high-performing people. Ask questions every chance you get. Don't just settle for the status quo.

5. Eliminate wasted time in meetings.

Harvard Professor Nancy Koehn estimates that eleven million meetings are held each day in the US.[9]

Again, I realize you may not have control over which meetings you have to attend. But even though you may not be in charge, you can still help the meetings to be fruitful and productive. Think through meetings by asking the following questions:

Who really needs to be there?

Is the meeting tactical or strategic?

What is the win?

What decisions do we need to make?

What is the best time of the day or week?

What can be handled offline?

How long does the meeting really need to be?

A company called Asana has "no meeting Wednesdays." This allows people to focus completely on their priority projects one day a week. I think most ministries and organizations could give their people back a few hours every month if they were just more disciplined with their meetings.

Sometimes I feel like the little boy with the loaves and fishes (see John 6:1–14). He didn't have much, but he wholeheartedly offered what he had. I may not be the most talented. And I may not be the most gifted. And maybe I don't have an impressive title or position or office. But Jesus says that if we just show up and step up, He will take what we have and multiply it. My challenge to you is to keep showing up. Get up every day and bring your A game to your ministry. I also challenge you to step up. Take your productivity to the next level. Improve. Get better. Not just so you can get more done and check off more boxes on your to-do list. But so you can participate more fully in the work God is doing in and through you.

This week may you get 'er done in Jesus's name.

TEAM DISCUSSION QUESTIONS

1. How do you need to rearrange your life and schedule to be more productive?

2. When you hear the challenge to "take outlandish control of your schedule," what is your response?

3. What difference would it make if you focused more on minutes and less on hours?

4. What could your teammates do to help you be more productive?

18

Techno-Danger

Hi, my name is Lance and I am a technology addict. This is the part of the group meeting where you say, "Hi, Lance." There is a certain irony that a few nights ago I was scrambling around the Charlotte, North Carolina, airport looking for an outlet so I could finish this chapter on my computer. I have this sort of love/hate relationship with all my gadgets. I love the convenience and the ways they make my life more efficient, but I hate how much they have invaded every nook and cranny of my life.

With the tsunami of techno-gadgets and apps, many of us struggle to not be consumed and controlled by technology. This reality has huge implications for us personally as well as for how we do team. And in the ministry world, always being plugged in not only can be seen as acceptable but also can be applauded because we are available, responsive, and connected.

I know I don't need to talk to you about the benefits of technology—and there are many. In terms of managing our lives, helping with the education of our kids, extending the reach of the gospel, or making our ministries more accessible, technology has been an incredible gift. We are experts at maximizing technology but not so good at managing it. We are good at leveraging technology but not so good at limiting it.

In this chapter, I want to share with you how we can avoid some of the subtle dangers of technology that can erode both health and high performance.

Virtual Instead of Personal Conversation

Technology is great for passing along information, but it is no substitute for personal conversation.

I wonder if there was ever a conversation that took place in heaven among the Trinity about when it would be best for Jesus to come. If there had been some tech savvy leader from the twenty-first century in that conversation, I'm sure the idea would have come up to skip the whole "incarnation" strategy. "Let's go virtual instead of incarnational." It would be much easier and more efficient to just do a webinar or live streaming.

Thank God, in His divine wisdom, Jesus came in the flesh. He walked among us and was with us. That's what the name Immanuel means—God with us.

And when it comes to doing team, for the sake of speed and efficiency, it is easy to default to always using technology. But there is something about face-to-face, in-the-flesh conversation that can never be replaced by technology.

Sherry Turkle, in her book *Reclaiming Conversation*, writes, "Without conversation, studies show that we are less empathetic, less connected, less creative and fulfilled."[1]

In ministry, not everything can be handled by text message or email. We must embrace the skill of in-person (incarnational) conversation.

Being Present in Conversation

Let me challenge you not to be distracted from the person who is there by the person who isn't there. When you read the Gospels, have you ever noticed that Jesus never seems to be distracted, preoccupied, or "checked out" when He is with someone?

Not too long ago, Connie and I went to dinner with some friends. No sooner had we sat down when they started getting text messages from their teenage kids. It wasn't any kind of emergency. It was just their having an ongoing text conversation with their kids while also having dinner with us. At least eight or ten times during the evening our conversation was disrupted by incoming text messages. I walked away feeling frustrated and devalued.

"What phones do to in-person conversation is a problem. Studies show that the mere presence of a phone on the table (even a phone turned off) changes what people talk about. If we think we might be interrupted, we keep conversations light, on topics of little controversy or consequence. . . . Even a silent phone disconnects us."[2]

When you are in a personal conversation, be present. Focus on the person in the room. Make eye contact and give them your full attention. And if for some reason you absolutely must respond to an incoming call or text, apologize and ask permission to do so.

Delivering Bad News

When you have to resolve a conflict or deliver hard news, don't use email, text, Twitter, or any other social media platform. Honestly, it is a very ineffective way to deal with a serious problem.

Technology is fine for sharing information, but it is terrible for confrontation. With email or text there is no opportunity for the person on the other end to see your body language or facial expressions. The other person can't hear your tone of voice. These forms of communication don't allow for real-time clarification and dialogue.

This has become a point of humor for my wife and me. Sometimes she will read a text to me that she has received. It is common for her to read tone or attitude into the text message. I have to remind her that it's possible to read the text with a totally different tone.

Technology has dehumanized communication. People hide behind a screen and now say things they would never say in person. It is the coward's way out of a hard conversation. We dishonor and devalue people when we fire off harsh emails and caustic text messages. And make no mistake about it—it creates dysfunction in a team environment.

Here's the challenge I want to give you. If you are dealing with a difficult issue, do it face-to-face, not screen-to-screen.

Establishing Technology Ground Rules

More and more companies are not allowing phones and computers in certain meetings. We have all been in meetings where it is obvious that people have checked out and are scrolling through email or looking at Pinterest or shopping on Amazon. I've also witnessed people hiding their phone out of sight under the table so they could respond to a text message without being noticed. Or somebody says they need a bathroom break, but they take their phone with them. It's remotely possible that I might have done some of these things myself.

But if we want people to stay engaged in meetings, we might need to help them by getting the techno-distractions out of the room.

Regarding the issue of techno-gadgets in meetings, a study done by USC's Marshall School of Business revealed the following information:

86 percent think it's inappropriate to answer calls during meetings.
84 percent think it's inappropriate to write texts or emails during meetings.
75 percent think it's inappropriate to read texts or emails during meetings.
It shows lack of respect, lack of attention, and lack of listening.[3]

Clarifying Technology Expectations

In your team culture, what is the expectation for responding to a text, answering an email, or returning a phone call? It is not fair to hold people to expectations that have never been clarified.

You might consider having a guideline that clarifies that you will respond to an email within twenty-four hours of having received it. One staff team I work with has a guideline that says if a matter is urgent, then pick up the phone and call the person rather than send an email or a text.

Another expectation that needs to be clarified has to do with evenings and people's days off. We all know that ministry is not a nine-to-five job. But how available are people expected to be when they are at home with their family or enjoying a day off? Different ministries will answer that question differently, but what's most important is that the expectations are clear.

Being Personal and Warm

The very nature of technology is that it is cold and sterile. A little bit of effort is required to make emails and texts feel more human. When communicating through technology, I always choose casual and personal over formal and professional. But it is possible to be both high tech and high touch. In fact, you can use your technology to help you be high touch.

You might consider having an electronic calendar that keeps track of important days. As an example, you might want to keep up with the birthdays of all the team members or volunteers in your ministry. You can set an alert to notify you a day or two ahead of their birthday. Then you can send an e-card on their birthday. In this impersonal world, a little bit of personal touch goes a long way.

Holy and Appropriate Technology Use

The truth is, a lot of worthless content makes the rounds in social media—off-color jokes, political rantings, preacher bashing, tasteless videos, etc.

A while back I got involved in a situation where a ministry wanted to hire a young, gifted leader. I think everyone thought the vetting was just a formality. However, one person in the process let it be known that he was against hiring this young leader. A year earlier this young leader had posted a bit of a rant on social media and this person was offended at both the post's stance and tone. The young leader responded humbly, and eventually it all got worked out and they hired him. But it was painful walking through the process and almost cost the young leader the job.

What he posted wasn't sinful, but it lacked good discretion and good judgment.

Realize that every single thing you post or tweet or email either builds or hurts your testimony. Because you are a leader in a Christian ministry, people will even pay attention to what you "like" on social media.

Another thing that raises the stakes for this issue is that once you post something online, it is a permanent record. You can't take it back. Ever.

Use wisdom and think before you post.

Technology for Encouragement and Prayer

Most of the practical applications I've shared have been warnings. But this practical idea is a way you can use technology to be a blessing.

A quick email to let someone know how much you appreciate them can make a huge difference. A three-line text to a teammate to celebrate the great job they are doing means more than you will ever know.

Often when I pray for people, I will shoot them a quick text to let them know the Lord had laid them on my heart and I am interceding on their behalf. Sometimes I will just type out the prayer I am praying on someone's behalf and then email it to them.

How Do We Get Better at Managing Our Technology?

Know yourself and your tendencies.

Where do you struggle with technology?

I like keeping my email inbox down to as few emails as possible. It feels like I am playing whack-a-mole all day long. I use Apple Mail, and a little red notification badge lets me know when I have received a new email. When I would see that little red circle pop up on my toolbar, it was like crack cocaine. I couldn't help myself. I had to see what new email had come to my inbox, because after all, Amazon might be having a big sale I need to know about.

I remember a flight I took a couple of years ago. The guy sitting next to me also used Apple Mail. When I glanced over at his computer, I noticed he had 17,423 unread emails. I almost started hyperventilating. I have since gone into my settings and turned off almost all the notifications. Now I only see email when I go and check it.

What adjustment do you need to make to have healthier habits regarding your technology use? If you are having a hard time knowing what you need to change, just ask your teammates. They can probably give you some suggestions.

Give people around you permission to throw a penalty flag.

In healthy team cultures, we help each other get better. Occasionally all of us violate good etiquette or unintentionally blow people off because we are distracted by our technology. Ask the people who live and work with you to help you manage your technology.

Be intentional to create space and distance from technology.

Consider having a technology Sabbath where you literally and metaphorically "unplug" for the day. I heard of one ministry leader who has a "go dark" week every year. Don't be surprised if you go through some withdrawal pains, but you will be better for it.

Establish some technology guidelines for your team.

What steps can you take as a team to make sure you use technology in a healthy way? I know one team that takes a basket with them whenever they go to lunch, and when they sit down, everyone throws their phone into the basket. And anybody who picks up their phone before lunch is over has to buy lunch for the group.

Before you get back to your email and Twitter accounts, I want to ask you to do a two-minute exercise. Think back over the last week. What were your best moments? When were you most fulfilled? What were the moments that mattered most? When did you feel most alive? When did your soul swell up with gratitude?

I doubt any of the moments that really counted happened while you were staring at a screen.

TEAM DISCUSSION QUESTIONS

1. As you think about your own technology use, what is one unhealthy behavior or pattern?
2. When you think about your team's health, what are some subtle dangers of technology?
3. How can you and your team be both high tech and high touch?
4. What is a guideline your team needs to implement to manage technology in a healthier way?

PART 5

PRIORITIZE RELATIONSHIPS

How we treat one another and relate to one another matters. There is a direct link between relationships and results. When relationships are transactional rather than personal, a lot of sideways energy is spent simply managing the team's dynamics and dysfunction. In this section, we will discover how to put people first and create a culture of "one another."

19

People First

My wife's birthday is in early December, and she had always wanted to go to New York City during the Christmas season. We saved up our money, bought our airline tickets, and headed off to the Big Apple. I had scoured the internet and was able to score a great hotel room at the Crowne Plaza right next to Times Square. I was so excited to give Connie the birthday present of experiencing the magic of New York City during Christmas. To get the lay of the land, we decided to do the Big Bus New York tour on our first day. We were having a great time seeing the sights of the city, but the weather was cold, snowy, and generally miserable. By the end of the first day, Connie began to come down with flu symptoms.

When she woke up on the second day, she was still feeling sick. I asked her what she wanted to do in light of the fact that she was feeling ill. She said, "I think it would be wise for me to stay in today, and perhaps I'll feel good enough to go to the Broadway show tonight." So, we settled in to spend the day together in the room.

When housekeeping came to the door to clean the room, I met them and let them know my wife wasn't feeling well and we just needed some fresh towels. They handed us some towels and went on their way.

A couple of hours later, there was a knock on the door. I assumed it was housekeeping again. But at the door was someone from room service with a tray. I told him we hadn't ordered anything from room service. He said, "I know, but we wanted to send up a little something for Mrs. Witt." The tray was covered with a white linen cloth, and on the tray was a bowl of soup, fresh bread, a glass of water, and a single flower in a vase. Also on the tray was a card signed by the lady from housekeeping. The card read, "There's no place like home when you're not feeling well. We hope this helps you feel a little better while you're in our home." We were blown away. We had never been treated with such personal care by a staff member at a hotel.

I remember thinking, *If the Crowne Plaza can treat people with such value and care, why can't the church of Jesus Christ do the same?*

One quality that sets apart great teams is the love and thoughtful care the members demonstrate to one another. To focus only on goals, objectives, and vision is shortsighted. Churches and organizations ought to lead the way in building team cultures that are defined by love. I know it is not okay with Jesus to be wildly successful externally and have a dysfunctional, toxic team environment.

As I work with churches and teams across the country, I am regularly asked, "How do you know if a team is healthy?" That's a great question. Diagnosing the health of a church or organization is certainly more art than science. But if you were going to hold your spiritual stethoscope to a ministry and listen for what's going on inside, the place I would start would be the staff/leadership culture.

I know this for sure. You can't diagnose the health of a ministry by its size or rate of growth. If you want to talk about the true spiritual health of an organization, you have to look at the health of the team that leads the organization.

A few years ago Connie and I attended a marriage conference with some friends. A few days later I sat down over coffee with the other husband to debrief the conference. He knew Connie and me very well. I asked him this question: "What do you think I could do to make Connie feel more valued?"

That seemed like a fair question, and I was rather proud of myself for taking the initiative to ask it. I expected us to brainstorm a few ideas that would enhance our marriages. But my friend's answer was not at all what I had expected and completely caught me off guard. He said, "Well, maybe if you actually start valuing her more, she will *feel* more valued." *Ouch!*

You see, I was looking for technique and strategy, and my friend was wise enough to point me back to my own heart.

Technique and strategy have their place in this discussion, but I think the right place to start is the heart. Do you love the people on your team? Let that question wash over you for just a minute. Do you really love the people whom you lead or serve with? If you were put on trial and the charge was not authentically loving your team, what evidence could be submitted? What would witnesses who work with you say? What would be exhibit A to show the jury?

You can be an effective leader and not love people. No, that's not a typo. You really can be an effective leader who moves the organizational ball down the field and not really love people. History is filled with gifted, dynamic leaders who steamrolled people on their way to success.

But you can't be an effective, Jesus-like leader and not love those on your team. In the words of Martin Luther King Jr., "Power [leadership] without love is reckless and abusive."[1] Just mark it down. When you have leadership without love, a wake of hurt and dysfunction follows.

In our leadership-intoxicated Christian culture, it is probably helpful for us to be reminded that the Bible has far more to say about love than leadership. What if we put the same time and energy into being loving and relational as we do ambitiously achieving our organizational goals?

Jewish tradition teaches that 613 laws were handed down from God to Moses in the Torah. These laws covered all aspects of life: family life, diet, clothing, sex, business relationships, religious celebrations, and many more. You can see why trying to obey everything God had commanded was an overwhelming proposition. One day, an expert in this Old Testament law came to Jesus and asked this question: "Which is the greatest commandment in the Law?" (Matt. 22:36). Jesus said the greatest commandments were to love God and love people (see vv. 37–39). Your highest calling is not to serve God and lead people or to obey God and make a difference in this world. Your highest and holiest calling is to love God and love people. If you deeply, authentically believed that, how would it change how you live your week and how you treat your team?

And then Jesus said, "All the Law and the Prophets hang on these two commandments" (Matt. 22:40). In other words, if we loved perfectly, there would be no need for the six hundred-plus laws. If we really loved God with our whole heart, we would never chase after idols or put our will before His. And if we really loved people, we would never harm, slander, manipulate, or diminish them.

I believe the same thing is true for our teams. If we could learn to truly love one another, so many other things I talk about in this book would be irrelevant. The Bible's message about loving people is relentless. In fact, in John 13, Jesus gives the world the right to judge the authenticity of our faith on how well we love one another: "By this everyone will know that you are my disciples, if you love one another" (John 13:35).

I would challenge you and your teammates to demonstrate personal care toward one another. I think the old saying really is true that people don't care how much you know until they know how much you care. That means you value your teammates for who they are as people gloriously created in the image of God, not just what they can do for you or the organization.

In a healthy, loving team, what matters most is not what we want from others but what we want for them. And what we want for them is a strong marriage, time with their kids, a healthy rhythm of life, and a genuine and vibrant walk with God. In a loving team environment, personal care for a team member sometimes needs to trump the ministry agenda.

Over the last two or three months, I have not been able to shake a passage of Scripture that I read in my quiet time. I think its simplicity and straightforward instruction were what struck me so profoundly. It is a passage containing just two short verses tucked into the last chapter of 1 Corinthians. As Paul wraps up his long letter to a very troubled church, he leaves them with some parting words that are so simple, they are impossible to misunderstand: "Be on guard. Stand firm in the faith. Be courageous. Be strong. And do everything with love" (1 Cor. 16:13–14 NLT).

Not easy to obey, but certainly simple to grasp. When I read this a few weeks ago, I remember thinking to myself, *If I could just live out these words, my life will be successful in God's eyes.* I am especially struck by the last challenge Paul gives: *Everything you do must be done with love.* The one nonnegotiable of how we deal with people is that we must love them. If that statement is true for people in general, it certainly should be true of those we call teammates.

For many of us, the desire to love and shepherd people is part of what God used to draw us to ministry. But somewhere along the way we got busy building a church or an organization. Time began to be consumed with planning and managing budgets and attending meetings and implementing strategy and running programs, and we forgot that our highest priority is to love people.

Let's raise our game when it comes to loving our team. If the Crowne Plaza can do it, so can we.

TEAM DISCUSSION QUESTIONS

1. Do you really love the people on your team? What is the evidence of your love?

2. What gets in the way of your being more loving to those you work with?

3. What can you do to demonstrate extravagant love to those you serve with?

4. In what ways can your team members communicate and demonstrate love to you?

20

The Slow Dance
of Building Trust

It was an awkward moment. I was sitting at dinner with a couple I have known for many years. While we weren't best friends, we had done ministry together for several years and felt mutual respect for one another. While we were eating our salads and having casual conversation, they let me know they wanted to talk to me about something.

Uh-oh! Warning alert! I've had lots of people over the years say those words to me, and what follows is never a compliment. They let me know they had said something to me that they thought was in confidence and were concerned I hadn't kept our conversation private. I shared something with their senior leader that they didn't think I should have.

As the Replenish guy, I have many personal conversations, and I have to be impeccable when it comes to holding confidences. I was definitely rattled by their accusation. I'm grateful they came to me personally so we could talk about it. We had a redemptive conversation, but I walked away knowing their trust in me had taken a hit. Fortunately, my track record with them had been good, and I had made lots of trust deposits. But at least in that moment there was a significant trust withdrawal. The next time we talked, I am sure they were more guarded about what they said.

As I was thinking about this issue of trust, it dawned on me that in ministry trust is our currency. Our congregations and the people who follow us trust us to lead them spiritually. Our credibility with our teammates is built on trust.

Having trust on a team is a gift. It paves the way for strong relationships, a healthy working environment, and notable productivity. But when it is missing, it creates dysfunctional working relationships, a suspicious working environment, and a loss of productivity.

In his book *The Five Dysfunctions of a Team*, Patrick Lencioni writes, "Trust lies at the heart of a functioning, cohesive team. Without it, teamwork is all but impossible."[1] Let that last sentence soak in—*without trust, teamwork is all but impossible.*

And without teamwork, we aren't as effective as we could be. High trust makes high performance possible.

It's not just right and healthy to create a high-trust working environment; it's highly effective and productive. When people feel comfortable and safe, they can be themselves and throw themselves completely into their work. In a low-trust environment, instead of people's energy being focused on their work, part of it gets siphoned off into figuring out how to navigate the dysfunctional environment.

I know trust is a little squishy. It is hard to quantify and measure. It is more of an environment or atmosphere than an activity. Trust likely never shows up on a personal performance review. And no one ever puts "build trust with my team" on their daily to-do list. More than a "to do," it is a dance—a slow dance.

Trust Equals Speed

"Trust equals speed," he said
Explaining why we need
To trust at work. Trust
Lets us move ahead
With lightning speed.
I think he's right.

Yet trust takes time.
It's silent, too,
And meditative in its

Steps. It moves at
Paces that seem slow
And hesitating,
First one foot,
Then the next.

Trust is a dance
Developed over time,
A set of natural steps
Emerging from a bond
Forged from passion
That we feel for dreams
We hold in common,
And respect
For all the ways we're not alike,
Both hold, the dreams and difference,
Unflinching and aware,
Day after day,
As we work
Side by side.

Trust equals speed.
Yet it is utterly,
Completely still.
Trust is unmoving
And it is the speed
Of light.

Judy Brown[2]

What a beautiful description of the slow dance of building a high-trust culture. Establishing trust is incremental, but the results can be exponential.

While the concept of trust can be squishy and it is a dance, it is a dance we can learn. And just like taking dance lessons, we can take movements and steps to not only learn the skill of dance but also enjoy it.

I want to talk about three steps in the dance of trust that can make it beautiful and enjoyable. And then I want to talk about three missteps that can make the dance ugly and unenjoyable.

Trust Builders

1. Be trustworthy.

Trust is built first by being trustworthy. Whenever the topic of trust comes up, our default mode is to look at the others on the team and determine what they do to contribute to or take away from trust. But the place you should start is with yourself—both personally and professionally. Introspectively evaluate your own actions and behaviors.

I think it is helpful to ask yourself the following questions:

- Am I acting in trustworthy ways?
- Am I reliable? Do I always do what I say?
- Do I "own it" when I mess up?
- Do I speak well of my teammates?
- Do I show up on time?
- Do I cheer on my teammates?
- Do I follow through?
- Do I treat teammates with honor and dignity?
- Do I show respect for those in authority over me?
- Am I always honest?
- Am I a good steward of my role and resources?
- Do I show up with a good attitude and bring my A game every day?

2. Demonstrate authentic care.

This makes me think of the apostle Paul speaking to the church at Philippi. He speaks in very affectionate terms about them. And then he writes, "So it is right that I should feel as I do about all of you, for you have a special place in my heart" (Phil. 1:7 NLT). Could you say the people on your team have a special place in your heart? Authentic care and love always raise the level of trust.

Part of authentic care is working hard to create an environment that feels "safe" for people. This means not having a hidden agenda, not throwing them under the bus in conversations, ensuring that their opinion is heard and respected, and treating them with honor both privately and publicly.

When an environment feels safe, people will begin to be more open and vulnerable.

To the list of steps you can take to demonstrate authentic care you can add being an attentive listener. So often we are preoccupied or jumping ahead without fully listening and just being present. When your teammates are speaking, give them your full and focused attention. Put down your phone. Make eye contact. Also, be authentically interested in them. Show interest in and care for their marriage, their kids, their pace, their workload, and their hobbies.

Finally, practice good relational and emotional skills. Don't fall into reading people's minds. Don't be passive-aggressive.

3. Help others win.

Helping others win is huge for elevating trust. Your support for others in the organization has direct correlation to trust. When they believe you are truly "for" them, their trust in you goes up. When they sense you believe in them and are cheering them on, their trust in you rises. When they see you are willing to do whatever you can to help them or their team succeed, that is a trust deposit.

This is the opposite of a self-protecting silo mentality. Patrick Lencioni says, "Silos are nothing more than the barriers that exist between departments within an organization, causing people who are supposed to be on the same team to work against each other. And whether we call this phenomenon departmental politics, divisional rivalry, or turf warfare, it is one of the most frustrating aspects of life in any sizable organization."[3]

Picture in your mind the grain silos that dot the landscape of the Midwest. These silos sit right next to each other, so there is proximity but no community. Each silo is self-contained, having no connection to or interaction or sharing with the other silos. These silos are closed off—no one can see what's going on inside. They have cold, hard walls designed to protect. What a great picture of what happens inside so many organizations, and when that is the reality, I promise you trust will be low.

It is not only important to identify the behaviors that build trust—it is critical to understand the actions that erode trust.

Trust Busters

1. Lack of honesty

Proverbs says, "The LORD detests lying lips, but he delights in people who are trustworthy" (Prov. 12:22). Notice how Solomon juxtaposes lying lips and being trustworthy.

When you shade the truth, spin your communication, or exaggerate your success, you undermine trust. Go ahead and decide right now that you are going to operate with integrity. Because moments will come when it will feel expedient to share only partial truths. There will be times when you will be tempted to tell the version of the story that makes you look good and somebody else look bad.

If you wait until you are in the heat of the moment to decide how you will react, you will usually make a bad decision. A question that has served me well through the years is, "What's the right thing to do?"

One great thing about integrity is that it reduces your options. Only those actions that are honest and reflect the character of God are open for consideration. It's kind of like the sinking of the *Titanic*. That epic disaster wasn't caused just by the ship colliding with an iceberg. The rest of the story has to do with the three million rivets that held the outer steel to the ship's hull. To save a little money, the company that built the *Titanic* used substandard iron. Consequently, the rivets were faulty and catastrophically failed. Life and teamwork are all about the rivets.

2. Insecurity

Doing the hard, internal soul work regarding your identity is crucial to building a culture of trust. To say it another way, when you are constantly plagued by insecurity, it lowers trust. We all struggle with insecurity at some level, but I'm talking about the pronounced insecurity that leaks into the team in negative and destructive ways.

You might be asking yourself, "What is the connection between insecurity and trust?" Insecure people have an incessant need to prove themselves. They often struggle with shame and a deep sense of inadequacy, and are driven to prove their worth and value. Rather than putting the focus on the team, they put the focus on themselves. Trust begins to break down because people on the team see that the insecure person will not always act in the best interest of the team. They will often act in their own best self-interest.

A common trait of an insecure person is that they need constant affirmation and recognition. Insecure people have a hard time with criticism, because it quickly makes them feel inadequate. All of these traits and behaviors have huge implications for trust among team members.

3. Dysfunctional organizational practices

A lot of ministry organizations and teams are like dysfunctional families, where members let bad behavior go without any kind of accountability or consequence. People eventually resign themselves to the reality of "it is what it is." But healthy ministries recognize that their organizational practices either help or hinder trust. Let me mention a couple of common practices I see that perpetuate dysfunction and erode trust.

Doing organizational work-arounds

Instead of following proper protocol or honoring the org chart, people go around their supervisor to make a request or get answers. If you are a leader in an organization, you are responsible for helping people honor the staff structure. When people run around the supervisor and come to you directly, you should always send them back to talk to their supervisor first.

Playing the position or title card

In ministry, you lead out of a place of relationship, servant leadership, and proven track record. When you power up and use positional authority, you may win the momentary battle, but ultimately you will lose the war. If you have to tell people you are the boss or remind them of your title, you will have low trust from the people on your team.

What to Do When Trust Has Been Broken

The truth is, trust will be broken. No matter how healthy or godly the culture, it is still filled with people who are broken and flawed. At some point you will break trust, and others will do something that will erode your trust in them. When that happens, sit down face-to-face and have a redemptive conversation. It is the only way to begin to repair the trust that has been broken. In such situations, I encourage you to seek restoration and ways to move forward. Even when you can't resolve the issue, you can restore the relationship. And remember:

Without trust we don't truly collaborate; we merely coordinate or, at best, cooperate. It is trust that transforms a group of people into a team.

Stephen Covey[4]

TEAM DISCUSSION QUESTIONS

1. What kind of grade would you give your team when it comes to vulnerability-based trust? Why?
2. What would it take to raise the level of trust in your ministry?
3. What do you want and need from your team?
4. When it comes to your team, what can feel "deflating" to you?

21

Crafting a Culture
of "One Another"

We live in a time when verbal attacks and public character assassinations are the order of the day. It seems that every political election is marked by accusations and innuendo. Mudslinging and exploitation appear to be the preferred strategy. The result: we have lost our sense of civility, and no person and no position is off-limits.

The advent of technology has compounded the problem. All our gadgets have made it easier for us to be vicious toward one another. We can now verbally assault people while hiding behind a screen. When we hold up this topic of crafting a culture of one another against the backdrop of twenty-first-century America, it is not just countercultural, it is radically countercultural. And sadly, it is too often counter to ministry culture.

I have chosen the word *crafting* very intentionally. When an artisan crafts something, skill, focus, patience, diligence, and a meticulous attention to detail are required. We will never accidentally create a culture of one another.

A ministry team environment is a great laboratory and testing ground for creating this kind of healthy relational culture. The signature verse for this topic has to be Romans 12:10: "Be devoted to one another in love. Honor one another above yourselves." *Be devoted to one another*. Those words are a mandate to every Christ-follower. We are to be committed to one another. We are not just devoted to the mission or the cause. We are not just devoted to our church or organization. We are not just devoted to the visionary leader. We are devoted to one another.

When we are devoted to one another, our relationships are personal rather than transactional. When our focus is personal, our first concern is for others. When our focus is transactional, our first concern is for ourselves and what others can do for us.

Transactional	Personal
Short-term view	Long-term view
People's value is extrinsic	People's value is intrinsic
Focused on the ends only	Focused on the means and the ends
Project focused	Person and project focused
Utilitarian	Trinitarian

If we are only transactional in our leadership, people will end up feeling used and devalued.

One day I was doing a life plan for a business leader, and we were working on the Life Net tool. It is a construct that identifies the web of our closest relationships. These are people who know us well, can speak honestly into our lives, and can support us in our pursuit to live out our life plan. As we were working on this exercise, this guy's wife walked in, so we reviewed the tool with her and asked her if we should consider any other names for his life net.

As soon as his wife mentioned a certain man's name as a possible candidate for his life net, the husband immediately responded, "No way. The only time he ever has anything to do with me is when he wants something from me." In other words, this man was saying that their relationship was not personal; it was only transactional. This guy knew his so-called friend's only interest in him was what he could get from him. When a relationship is transactional, a culture of one another will be MIA.

It never feels good in a relationship when our only value is what we can do for the other person. That's not just true in a marriage; it is also true in a ministry team environment. In a culture of honor, our approach to people is to be Trinitarian, not utilitarian. Think about the relationship within the Trinity. God the Father, God the Son, and God the Spirit coexist in harmony, alignment, unity, and mutual purpose. Each person of the Godhead is distinct in personality, but they care for and honor one another.

The end of Romans 12:10 says, "Honor one another above yourselves." But what does it look like to honor one another above ourselves? One accurate translation of this phrase in Romans 12:10 is to "lead the way in honoring others above yourself." The English Standard Version translates this phrase as "outdo one another in showing honor."

I love that because it is the opposite of our normal competitive spirit. Our human nature competes to show we are the best and to demonstrate we are number one. When we compete, it's usually about "us." But Paul says, "If you want to compete, be competitive in showing honor." Our ministries should be the very best at treating people with tender care and honor.

Two Foundational Building Blocks

There are two foundational building blocks for crafting a culture of honor, and the first one may be a bit of a surprise.

1. A culture of one another starts with how we view ourselves.

How we think about ourselves will actually determine our ability to love others. One critical building block to a culture of one another has to do with being secure in who we are in Christ. If that is a settled reality in our lives, we don't need to prove our worth and value. When we know that we are unconditionally accepted by Jesus, we don't have to spend all our energy trying to get others to accept us. We don't need to posture or turn the spotlight on us.

Insecurity destroys a spirit of one another. When we are insecure, we always have to make everything about us. We have all been around people whose deep insecurities cause them to turn all conversations back to themselves. Somehow, no matter what the topic, the conversation always ends up being about them. A lack of emotional health will always become a roadblock to a culture of one another.

When our inward lives are secure, we can turn our focus outward.

I have also noticed that fatigue and busyness erode a healthy relational team culture. When we are compulsively busy, we are too distracted and preoccupied to give much attention to honoring others. And when we are exhausted and running on empty, we become irritable and don't have anything to give others.

I remember one night flying back home to the Denver airport. Our flight had been delayed, and we didn't land until 11:30 p.m. in a snowstorm. We then sat on the tarmac for forty minutes waiting for a gate. When we were finally assigned a gate, we had to wait thirty minutes for a gate agent to maneuver the jet bridge to the plane. I finally got my luggage close to 1 a.m. and headed to catch the hotel shuttle. I had decided to stay at an airport hotel rather than try to drive home that night.

In this comedy of errors, the next thing that happened was that the shuttle driver drove right past me. I then called the hotel and couldn't reach anyone. But I did get the hotel voicemail, so in an irritated tone of voice, I left them a very unpastoral message. I know. I was a jerk. Did I mention that fatigue erodes honor? But when we show up each day emotionally healthy and filled up with Jesus, a culture of one another is possible.

2. A culture of one another is about how we view others.

A culture of honor puts people first, ahead of projects. Even in ministry organizations that are people focused, it is possible to let our projects and initiatives and systems and tasks get in the way of our valuing the very people we work with. Bill Hybels is accurate when he writes, "It stands to reason, then, that a leader sometimes seems to be three-fourths steamroller and one-fourth caring and compassionate colleague. When a leader walks into a meeting, for example, he or she usually has only one thing on the brain: mission advancement."[1]

If you are a hard-driving leader, you will be tempted to trample on a culture of one another in the name of accomplishing the vision. I'm not saying that in a culture of one another you spend all your energy trying to appease people and keep everyone happy. What I'm talking about is that in your pursuit of the vision God has given you, make sure to treat people with dignity, respect, value, and care. And don't mistreat, manipulate, or "use" people.

One distinguishing characteristic of a Jesus organization is that we are not just people of the "ends"; we are people of the "means." We don't just care about accomplishing a vision or a goal; we care about how it gets done. We must care about the how as much as the what. I truly believe that Jesus cares just as much about how we treat people along the path to our vision as He does about accomplishing it.

One way we can do that is to put a number 10 on everybody's forehead. This is about training ourselves to see every person as Jesus sees them. No matter what position a person holds on our team or organization, we should put a number 10 on their forehead.

A culture of one another not only puts people ahead of projects, but it also appreciates the beauty of diversity. This is beautifully illustrated in 1 Corinthians 12:21–23: "The eye cannot say to the hand, 'I don't need you!' And the head cannot say to the feet, 'I don't need you!' On the contrary, those parts of the body that seem to be weaker are indispensable, and the parts that we think are less honorable we treat with special honor."

Paul says that those in prominent positions should take special care to show appreciation of and honor to those who hold less prominent positions in the body. Prominence does not equal significance, and visible does not mean more valuable. Any sensible person is more concerned with their heart than their hair. In a culture of one another, the most visible team members aren't any more important than the least visible team members.

Paul says we treat people with value "so that there should be no division in the body, but that its parts should have equal concern for each other" (v. 25). When we craft a culture of one another, we maximize unity and minimize division. When we craft a culture of one another, we have equal concern for each person.

There is a beautiful picture of the spirit of one another in the Old Testament. One day King David remembered a conversation he had twenty years earlier with his good friend Jonathan. In that conversation they promised they would always show kindness to each other and each other's families. But Jonathan had been tragically killed in battle years earlier, and in those days any remaining family members of a deposed king were quickly executed to put down any chance of an uprising.

After Jonathan's death, everyone in the palace had begun to flee, fearing for their lives. A nurse picked up Jonathan's five-year-old son, Mephibosheth, and tried to run out of the palace. However, in the confusion and panic, she fell, and young Mephibosheth was crippled for life (see 2 Sam. 4:4).

On that fateful day of his father's death, this little boy's entire destiny changed. One day he was running around the palace like any other five-year-old. The next day he was an orphan and a fugitive who was now crippled for life.

Twenty years later, David found Mephibosheth and had him brought to the palace. Mephibosheth was terrified. Before David could say anything, Mephibosheth fell to the floor and said, "I am your servant." But David's first words to him were filled with grace: "Don't be afraid." Then David surprised him with lavish grace.

But Mephibosheth, trying to make sense of the situation, said, "What is your servant, that you should notice a dead dog like me?" This unexpected display of honor had left him reeling. It was surreal. He was a nobody. He was a fugitive. He was crippled. He had absolutely nothing to offer.

David told Mephibosheth he would always be provided for and eat at the king's table. Mephibosheth, a crippled fugitive, was now being included in the royal family.

Imagine this scene a few months later. The dinner bell rings through the king's palace and David comes to the head of the table and sits down. Each family member quickly takes their seat. But there is still an empty seat. They wait. They hear the shuffling of feet, the slow movement of crutches. It is Mephibosheth gradually making his way to the table. He awkwardly slips into his seat and eats as one of the king's children.

Do you think Mephibosheth understood a culture of one another?

TEAM DISCUSSION QUESTIONS

1. What is one practical way you can "be devoted" to your team members?
2. What is one way you can honor your team members above yourself?
3. How can you up your game when it comes to putting a number 10 on everyone's forehead?
4. How well do you think your team members do at having equal concern for one another?

22

"One Another" Best Practices

If you are like me, you love the Olympics. But there is one Olympic event that doesn't get much press. It's the hundred-meter grocery cart dash.

Imagine you are in the grocery store. You are in a hurry (as always). You have picked up the eleven items on your list in less than three minutes. You are on pace for a record time getting out of the store. The only obstacle between you and the gold medal is the checkout stand. You spot an open checker with no one in line. Your heart races. You briskly push the cart to the open lane. You can sense the thrill of victory. Then out of nowhere a little old lady appears with a cart half full of groceries. Everything in you wants to stretch for the finish line (checkout stand), but you stop. Victory is snatched from you as you utter those words your mother taught you: "You first." Two simple words. Yet they capture the essence of Paul's command in Romans 12:10: "Be devoted to one another in love. Honor one another above yourselves."

What does a culture of one another in your team look like practically? How does it show up in a Tuesday morning conversation or a Thursday afternoon team meeting?

I believe three best practices facilitate a culture of one another.

Blessing

Blessing is all about how you talk to people. This practice is about the words that flow from you into the lives of others. Here's the great news. Anybody can be great at blessing. It doesn't require a certain level of skill or education. It's not dependent on your title or position in the organization. You don't need a budget line item to succeed in this practice. For minimal investment, there is amazing return.

Luke 24 records the final moments that Jesus spent on earth. He had been crucified, resurrected, and was ready to return to His rightful place in heaven. It is not surprising that He spent these final hours with His band of brothers.

Jesus obviously knew His ascension was imminent. If you were Jesus, and this was your final time to be with the disciples, what would you share with them? Perhaps Jesus could have given them His three-year strategic plan for His global vision. There had regularly been fighting and jockeying for position among the disciples, so He could have handed out an org chart so the disciples would have clarity on lines of authority. Since the church would be launched soon at Pentecost, perhaps it would have been wise for Jesus to pass out bylaws for how the church should function and be governed.

As important as each of those things might have been, that is not what Jesus did during these final moments on earth. Instead, "While [Jesus] was blessing them, he left them and was taken up into heaven" (Luke 24:51). The very last words from the lips of Jesus on this planet were words of blessing.

Every one of us can remember occasions where somebody spoke blessing into our life. They affirmed us, believed in us, encouraged us, and it gave us confidence and hope. Words of blessing have great power. That's why Solomon writes, "The tongue has the power of life and death" (Prov. 18:21).

Don't underestimate the power of your words. As a leader and team member, your words have staying power. Your comments get amplified. That's why it's so important that life-giving words flow freely and frequently from your lips.

How are you doing at speaking blessing? What kind of grade would you give yourself? How are you doing at speaking blessing to your team members and those in your ministry? Let me challenge you to work on consistently making deposits into people's emotional bank accounts through words of blessing.

Here is a short list of practical ways you can bless people and help craft a culture of one another:

- listen attentively
- be fully present in a conversation
- ask someone to share their personal story
- show interest in someone's family
- celebrate others' victories
- see the good and God in people
- notice the little things
- personally care for someone in a crisis

Which one of these are you doing well? Maybe consider circling the one you want to work on in this coming week.

Most teams I have been around are comprised of good-hearted, kind, and caring people. It is my observation that the biggest barrier to words of blessing is not insensitivity, selfishness, lack of concern, or mean-spirited team members. The single biggest roadblock I see is speed. Speed and hurry will always diminish a culture of one another. When you go fast, you tend to miss the small opportunities to speak blessing. When your pace is accelerated, you're tempted to become more task oriented and less people oriented.

Protecting

Blessing is all about how you speak *to* people, while protecting is how you talk *about* people. In a culture of one another, what your teammates feel from you is that you've got their back. When you're in conversation and their name comes up, they can count on you to protect them and their reputation.

First Peter 4:8 gives us this challenge: "Above all, love each other deeply, because love covers over a multitude of sins." Most scholars believe this verse in 1 Peter is referring back to Proverbs 10:12, which says, "Hatred stirs up conflict, but love covers over all wrongs." When people have animosity toward someone, Solomon says they will stir up conflict. Instead of overlooking an issue, they feel compelled to agitate and make known the issue they are upset about. In contrast, Solomon says that love covers all wrongs. Love protects, forgives, and chooses to overlook. When you cover over something, you don't expose it.

Are you a "stir up" or "cover over" kind of teammate?

Years ago I was participating in a mission trip. A group from another church was also there that week. One night after we had done mission projects all day, we decided to have a friendly game of volleyball between the two churches. During the game, one of the young ladies from the other church fell to the floor and began to convulse violently. It was obvious to everyone she was having a seizure of some kind. A handful of people gathered around her to try to figure out how to best help her. When she had fallen to the ground, her sweatshirt had gotten pulled up and now her midsection was exposed.

One of her friends went to the bleachers and found a spare sweatshirt. As some of the leaders were huddled over this young lady having a seizure, her friend came over and gently laid the sweatshirt over her midsection. She knew her friend would be embarrassed to be exposed, so she tenderly "covered over" the problem.

What a beautiful picture of what the members of healthy teams do for one another. When someone has a bad day, we "cover over" the situation with love. When someone disagrees with us, we don't throw them under the bus in a conversation with another team member. When someone on the team screws up, rather than gossiping about it, we gently cover over the situation with grace. We don't expose our friends to embarrassment and humiliation.

In a culture of one another, when we speak of others, we wouldn't mind if they were standing there listening to our words. We speak about people just as we would speak to them.

Interceding

Inevitably, if you stay around long enough, you will have a hard time honoring someone on the team or in the organization. Maybe your personalities clash or perhaps this person grates on your nerves. It could be that they pick apart every idea you have or they dominate meetings or you don't agree with their leadership style. They are like heavenly sandpaper—and they just grind on you.

I wouldn't be surprised if somebody's name just came to your mind. And when you think about your last encounter with them, it still irritates you. You guys are never likely to be best buddies, but you have to work together on the same team. How do you create a culture of one another when you have a teammate who drives you crazy?

Pray for them. Seriously. Now, I'm not talking about the kind of prayer that says, "Okay, God, get 'em." I'm talking about authentically lifting their name before the Lord and praying for God's blessing and favor on their life. Personally, I find that when I intercede for someone, my heart becomes softer toward them.

First Peter 4:7 says, "The end of all things is near. Therefore be alert and of sober mind so that you may pray." Peter says that time and history as we know it are winding down. But I'm a little surprised by the next statement in verse 7. I would have thought Peter would say that he wants us to pray so we will be alert and sober minded. But he says just the opposite. He wants us to be spiritually alert and clear minded so we can pray. Here is the point I think Peter is making. When we are truly spiritually alert and thinking clearly, we will understand that prayer is the most important thing we can do.

According to Paul, "the weapons we fight with are not the weapons of the world" (2 Cor. 10:4). When we have our spiritual antennas up, we realize that prayer is one of the most powerful spiritual weapons we have. If Satan can cause division or blow up your team, he can undermine the effectiveness of your ministry. And if he can't blow up your team, he is happy to keep you distracted with a dysfunctional team dynamic.

When a team has dysfunction and conflict, gaps get created in relationships. In the UK, the subway is referred to as the Tube. Whenever you ride the Tube, you see signs everywhere on the train platform that say, "Mind the gap." The gap is that little bit of space between the platform and the train. The gap is dangerous. If you don't pay attention to the gap, you could get hurt.

When it comes to crafting a culture of one another, you must learn to mind the gap. The health of the team depends on what you do with the gap. In many teams, when there is a relational gap, people fill it with suspicion, resentment, anger, and gossip. The result is that the relational gap gets bigger.

If you truly want to create a culture of one another, you must learn to fill the gap with prayer. What if the next time you are having a hard time honoring someone or they are driving you crazy, you turn to the Lord instead of an uninvolved friend?

What is God saying to you right now? As a team member, which of the three practices highlighted in this chapter do you need to work on in the coming weeks? A culture of one another is built by people who bless, protect, and intercede for their team members. Own it. *Be* the change you want to see in your organization. And remember, you don't have to have a position of influence to be a person of influence.[1]

TEAM DISCUSSION QUESTIONS

1. When did somebody meaningfully speak blessing into your life?
2. Which of the following do you need to put into practice?

   - listen attentively
   - be fully present in a conversation
   - ask someone to share their personal story
   - show interest in someone's family
   - celebrate others' victories
   - see the good and God in people
   - notice the little things
   - personally care for someone in a crisis

3. What are some practical ways you can protect your team members?
4. If you were explaining a culture of one another to a friend, what would you say?

23

The Big Brother Syndrome

As a communicator, I absolutely love to talk about a specific handful of topics. I get energized when I have the opportunity to speak about them. This is *not* one of those topics. The content of this chapter comes much more from a place of obedience and conviction. If you are reading this chapter looking for a warm, fuzzy, goose-bump, pick-me-up message, then let me go ahead and dash your hopes right now.

But I hope you will keep reading because I believe this is a timely word for our generation. And a timely word for every team.

Over the last decade, what one word or phrase would you use to label our generation? Think about that question for a moment. If you could take our last ten years of history and write one word to describe our culture, what word would you choose?

The word I want to talk about in this chapter would certainly make my list of top words that would characterize our generation. It is the word *entitlement*.

Entitlement is an attitude, feeling, or belief that you have a "right" to something. The word *deserve* is a cousin to entitlement. John Townsend defines it as the "belief that I am exempt from responsibility and I am owed special treatment."[1]

I think you would agree that a spirit of entitlement is epidemic in our culture. And it is not limited to any one age or demographic. We are maybe the most self-absorbed generation in the history of the world. It's seen in our welfare mind-set, our itch to sue everyone, our trophy-child parenting, and our incessant obsession with rights. It's seen in celebrities and athletes. We can observe it in students and politicians. And, yes, we can find it in our churches and ministry organizations.

Let's take a few minutes to unpack what the Bible has to say about this issue. You won't read the word *entitlement* in Scripture, but the issue is addressed countless times.

Now, let me take you through a passage you have probably never heard a sermon based on.

> Suppose one of you has a servant plowing or looking after the sheep. Will he say to the servant when he comes in from the field, "Come along now and sit down to eat"? Won't he rather say, "Prepare my supper, get yourself ready and wait on me while I eat and drink; after that you may eat and drink"? Will he thank the servant because he did what he was told to do? So you also, when you have done everything you were told to do, should say, "We are unworthy servants; we have only done our duty." (Luke 17:7–10)

That last phrase is the anti-entitlement verse in the Bible. *We are unworthy servants. We have only done our duty.* There is no demanding of rights or deserving special treatment. There is nothing especially grand or noble about slaves doing what slaves are supposed to do. It's their job to serve. According to verse 9, slaves don't deserve any kind of special recognition or thanks because they simply have fulfilled their responsibility.

Now you might be sitting there thinking to yourself, *But I remember when Jesus said He no longer calls us servants but friends. And Paul said I was adopted into God's family, and I'm a co-heir with Jesus. Paul said I'm God's masterpiece, created for good works. I'm special.*

So, what's up with the slave language? It's not either/or. It's both/and. I think it's healthy for us to be reminded that we are slaves to Jesus in addition to being adopted as sons and daughters. Slaves aren't the captain of their own destinies. Slaves don't own anything. Slaves don't have rights.

Slaves are 100 percent dependent on their masters. Slaves aren't entitled to anything.

By the way, Paul uses this imagery over and over again in his writings. And when you read the word *servant*, most often it is a translation of the Greek word *doulos*, which is most accurately translated as "slave."

We are slaves who have been given the unbelievable blessing of sonship. We are not sons who have been given the unpleasant burden of servitude. There is a huge difference between those two statements. The first statement breaks entitlement. The second statement breeds entitlement.

How might it impact your team dynamic if everyone showed up each day as simply a slave of Jesus? It was St. Francis of Assisi who said, "Blessed is he who expects nothing, for he shall enjoy everything."[2]

We all know the famous story of the prodigal son (see Luke 15:11–32). It is a classic story of God's patient love and extravagant grace. But when you read the passage carefully, you discover that the story has more than one prodigal son. Within this beautiful story is a subplot of a resentful older brother who plays the victim and embodies a spirit of entitlement.

I would encourage you to read the following passage out loud. And when you do so, read it with some "attitude." Insert a dash of resentment and a sprinkle of outrage and you will have the tone of the older brother.

After the prodigal son returned home and a party was being thrown on his behalf, we read:

> The older brother became angry and refused to go in. So his father went out and pleaded with him. But he answered his father, "Look! All these years I've been slaving for you and never disobeyed your orders. Yet you never gave me even a young goat so I could celebrate with my friends. But when this son of yours who has squandered your property with prostitutes comes home, you kill the fattened calf for him!" (vv. 28–30)

This brief outburst from the older brother offers a picture of what entitlement looks like when it manifests itself. Notice first that the older brother has an inflated view of himself.

"All these years I've been slaving for you and never disobeyed your orders."

Really? This is what I would call "spin." I think the older brother slightly embellishes how good he has been and how hard his life has been. We all have this tendency.

In Deuteronomy 9, we read that the people of Israel were about to cross over the Jordan into the promised land. God promised to go before them and drive out their enemies. But then He gave Israel a warning: "After the LORD your God has done this for you, don't say in your hearts, 'The LORD has given us this land because we are such good people!'" (Deut. 9:4 NLT).

Three times in three verses He tells them their blessings were not because of their goodness. They would be tempted to have an inflated view of themselves and take credit for all the good things that were happening. And then God puts an exclamation point on the passage in verse 6:

> You must recognize that the LORD your God is not giving you this good land because you are good, for you are not—you are a stubborn people.

When you have an inflated view of yourself, you will begin to look down on others. And when you "spin" just how good you are, you will come across as prideful and arrogant to your teammates.

Not only did the older brother have an inflated view of himself, but he also engaged in scorekeeping and comparing. *But when this son of yours who has squandered your property with prostitutes comes home, you kill the fattened calf for him!*

The older brother said, "I'm the good son. All these years I've been faithfully working on the farm. I have never rebelled." When you are an older brother, you are always keeping score, making sure you are getting your due. Older brothers are obsessed with making sure their rights aren't trampled on, ensuring somebody else doesn't get what rightfully belongs to them.

Nothing good ever comes from scorekeeping and comparing. It leads to either discouragement, because somebody is always doing more and better, or it leads to pride, because you can always find someone who isn't doing as much as you are.

By the way, you might have the spirit of the older brother if expressions of grace or favor toward others produce grumbling in you, which is exactly what happens in the story of the prodigal son.

The older brother also has no joy. I've never met a person with a spirit of entitlement who was happy and joyful and content. Notice his language. *Look! All these years I've been slaving for you.* He didn't see the blessing he had; he saw the burden. He saw obligation and duty rather than gratitude and beauty.

I think this is one thing I am finally beginning to learn after all these years: to live from a place of gratitude. I serve God because I love him, not out of obligation or duty. When I serve out of love, it diminishes drudgery and increases joy.

One mark of entitlement is grumbling for what you don't have rather than showing gratitude for what you do have. How is your grumble meter these days?

If we are all honest, we can probably see ourselves in the older brother.

Five Practices to Battle Entitlement

1. Say no to your flesh.

My ability to say no to my flesh got tested in me not long ago. I was checking into a hotel late one night, but the hotel was very full and had given away my room to somebody else. I was already tired and a little grumpy, and this news didn't help. While the guy was working on the computer to find me a room in a nearby hotel, I had about a thirty-second conversation with the Lord. I had wanted to ask for a manager and let somebody know how many nights a year I stay in their hotel and that this was unacceptable. But then I felt a little nudge in my spirit that said, "Let it go, Lance. It's not a big deal, and actually it's good for you to say no to your flesh."

Learning to say no to your fleshly desires and expectations helps curb entitlement in your life.

This is about building your anti-entitlement muscle by passing the small, daily tests that come your way. It might be a meeting you didn't get invited to or someone taking the parking space you were about to pull into. It could be a poor customer service experience or someone getting a nicer workspace than you.

I know my bent toward entitlement will get tested several times a day and that it is good for my growth and character to regularly give up what I think are my "rights."

2. Stop blameshifting.

Wherever entitlement exists, blaming and whining will not be far behind. This issue is as old as the human race. When God asked Adam why he ate the forbidden fruit, Adam was quick to throw Eve under the bus. Eve, being a quick study, pointed the finger of blame at the wily serpent when God asked her why she had eaten the fruit.

Little is worse than a leader throwing their team under the bus while they move into self-protection mode. That destroys credibility with the team and smacks of pride.

"Humble leaders are willing to pass on the credit but absorb the criticism, push others higher while making themselves lower. . . . A leader's job is to shepherd, not necessarily to always shine."[3]

Be quick to own your mistakes and apologize without rationalization. You will do more damage by your stiff-necked unwillingness to admit wrong than any mistake you made in performing your role.

Mistakes are rarely as damaging to an organization as a refusal to concede mistakes and apologize.

When the author of Hebrews is talking about the role of the priest, he writes, "And he is able to deal gently with ignorant and wayward people because he himself is subject to the same weaknesses" (Heb. 5:2 NLT).

One way to raise your gentleness quotient toward your team is to be more in touch with your own weaknesses and mistakes.

3. Resist the temptation to self-promote.

Let someone else praise you, and not your own mouth. (Prov. 27:2)

Work hard at praising others and not yourself. Don't always be the hero of your own stories. Resist the temptation to manipulate a conversation so you can talk about yourself. Feeling the need to self-promote is a warning sign of being emotionally unhealthy. We all enjoy being affirmed and acknowledged and recognized. But when you do that for yourself, you end up coming across to your team members as insecure and needy.

A magnet for self-promotion is social media. When you combine a selfie generation with a tool like social media, it is a deadly cocktail. It is very easy to use social media to portray an embellished and exaggerated life. Stay away from the "humble brag" on social media.

While I'm already meddling, let me bring up one more sticky issue. And that is the common temptation for people in ministry to exaggerate. To be seen as a success, we can be tempted to fudge on our numbers and inflate the size of our ministry. I know I have been guilty of this, and we all know it is a common issue in ministry. Let me challenge you and your team to be ruthlessly accurate when describing your ministry.

4. Make much of Jesus.

Speak of Jesus often. Brag on Him. Lift Him up. Make His name famous and don't worry about making your name famous. As John the Baptist said, "He must become greater and greater, and I must become less and less" (John 3:30 NLT).

I remember a few years ago being backstage at a conference where Chuck Swindoll was speaking. As a young pastor, I had read all of Swindoll's books and listened to hundreds of his sermons. So, it was a great honor to spend a few minutes with him. He was exactly as I had expected him to be. Chuck and my wife, Connie, grew up in the same part of Texas, and you would have thought they were long-lost friends. He was cordial, unpretentious, down-to-earth, and authentically interested in us. He had no entourage, no handler, and not a hint of the "big dog" persona.

It really is true; humility looks good on everyone. And it will look good on you and your team.

5. Serve your teammates.

Unselfishly serving others is a great way to keep entitlement at bay. And a very practical place to start is with those on your team.

Ever since the days of John 13, when Jesus washed the feet of the disciples, the towel has been a symbol of humble servanthood. It's not a symbol of power and money and position and status. It's a symbol of sacrifice and unselfishness and kindness and love for others. It's the anti-entitlement symbol.

In most everybody's house are two kinds of towels. There are the nice, clean, new towels hanging in the guest bathroom. Now, we all know we aren't supposed to use those towels. They are for decoration, for looking at. But as far as towels go, they are worthless. Towels are not made to be looked at; they are made to serve and to clean up messes.

Then there are the other towels—and every family has them. They're usually in the laundry room or even the garage. They're old, frayed around the edges, stained, and dirty. You don't hang these in the guest bathroom. You wash the car with these, you dry off the dog with these, you clean up a mess with these. These towels are not pretty. They are certainly not for decoration. But for what towels are made to do, they are perfect.

Let's pretend today that *you* are a towel. Here's the question: Are you an entitled guest-room towel or a garage-shelf towel? Let's make sure none of us show up in heaven having lived as a guest-room towel. Let's show up as a towel that is dirty, stained, and worn out from loving and caring for and serving people.

TEAM DISCUSSION QUESTIONS

1. Read back over the words of the older brother in Luke 15:28–30. What most stands out to you?

2. Where can entitlement worm its way into your thinking?

3. Of the five practices for battling entitlement, which one do you most need to put into play?

4. How can a spirit of entitlement become toxic to a team? As a team, how can you guard against a spirit of entitlement?

PART 6

DEFUSE LAND MINES

E very team and ministry has organizational land mines. We tend to ignore them until someone steps on one and causes an explosion, which usually includes collateral damage. We cannot ignore or live in denial about the hard things that come with doing team. In this section, we will talk about how to delicately and directly defuse volatile organizational land mines.

24

Getting Comfortable with Uncomfortable Conversations

It is a common practice in highly volatile regions of the world for NATO to send in peacekeeping troops. Those two words side by side can seem like an oxymoron. Peace and troops don't usually go together. These men and women are not politicians, educators, pastors, or economists. They are trained soldiers, and they are equipped to do battle. They are anything but passive observers. They literally fight for peace.

When it comes to pursuing peace in personal relationships or on a church team, you will have to skillfully fight for it. And just like those NATO peacekeeping troops, you must be equipped to accomplish the objective. This chapter and the next are about equipping you with practical strategies and tools so that you will be skilled in keeping the peace.

I love the words of Ephesians 4:3 where Paul challenges us to "make every effort to keep the unity of the Spirit through the bond of peace."

This is a command to every single believer. No matter what your role on the team or your position in the organization, you are called to make every effort to advocate and even fight for unity. This takes great vigilance and diligence. Peacekeeping troops are always on the alert for anything that might be a threat to peace.

Many church teams give the appearance of unity. The members are polite, friendly, and cordial, and there are no outward signs of conflict. But if you scratch beneath the surface or could hear private conversations, you would find resentment, gossip, cynicism, and the church version of trash-talking.

Instead of having uncomfortable conversations to resolve issues, they tap dance around the conflict. They make nice in the meeting but in private conversations are not so nice. Tension and dysfunction are often underneath the veneer of politeness.

Patrick Lencioni is spot-on when he writes that teams that don't engage conflict "resort to veiled discussions and guarded comments."[1]

In the opening chapter of *Crucial Conversations*, the authors make a dramatic declaration: "Twenty years of research involving more than 100,000 people reveals that the key skill of effective leaders, teammates, parents and loved ones is the capacity to skillfully address emotionally and politically risky issues. Period."[2]

And after more than forty years in ministry, I can conclude that this is an area where those of us in ministry have been woefully deficient.

Patrick Lencioni validates this reality. When talking about the propensity to avoid conflict, he says, "Nowhere does this tendency show itself more than in mission-driven nonprofit organizations, most notably churches. People who work in those organizations tend to have a misguided idea that they cannot be frustrated or disagreeable with one another."[3]

Instead of normalizing conflict, we have demonized it. Although there are times when conflict is divisive and harmful, much of conflict is about differing perspectives, personalities, and simply being part of a family or on a team.

But the cost of conflict avoidance is substantial. An inability to engage uncomfortable conversations can lead to the following:

- hurt feelings
- lost productivity
- unhealthy team culture
- lack of respect
- mistrust

- organizational dysfunction
- distraction from mission
- higher turnover
- gossip
- cynicism

The stakes really are high. *Crucial Conversations* highlights the story of a woman who checked into the hospital to have a tonsillectomy, and the surgical team erroneously removed a portion of her foot. Unbelievable. How could such glaring negligence actually happen? "In part because many health-care professionals are afraid to speak their minds. In this case, no less than seven people wondered why the surgeon was working on the foot, but said nothing."[4]

No one on your ministry team is losing an actual body part because uncomfortable conversations aren't happening, but the body of Christ does suffer damage when a team doesn't do this well. I encourage you to "lean in" on this topic. Remember, every single one of us is mandated to "make every effort to keep the unity of the Spirit." This is not reserved for department directors or those in senior leadership. It is the responsibility of every single person in the organization.

For his fascinating book *Guinea Pig Diaries*, A. J. Jacobs decided to put himself through a series of random experiments. For example, he lived a year completely adhering to all the Old Testament laws. In another experiment, he tried to see how much of his life he could outsource.

One experiment originated with an idea from a psychotherapist named Brad Blanton. The idea is called "radical honesty." Blanton says we would all be happier if we just quit lying. So he suggests tossing out the filter between our brains and our mouths. He believes it is the only path to authentic relationships.

As an experiment, Jacobs decided to always say "exactly what he was thinking in the moment." You can imagine how well that went over. Here is his conclusion: "I had to do some apologizing. . . . I've come to appreciate the filter between the brain and the mouth. Words can be dangerous."[5]

Having an uncomfortable conversation doesn't mean becoming a verbal wrecking ball or removing the filter between our thoughts and our words. And for the vast majority of us in ministry, that is far from our issue. In fact, we have just the opposite problem. We run from confrontation and conflict like they are the plague.

Nobody likes having the "uncomfortable conversation"—and if you do enjoy it, you probably shouldn't be in ministry. When you love people and have a shepherd's heart, uncomfortable conversations should cause a little angst and turmoil in your soul.

But there are times when, for the sake of relationships and vision, you must engage in an uncomfortable conversation. Such times make me think of Paul's challenge in Romans 12:18: "If it is possible, as far as it depends on you, live at peace with everyone." When I read that verse, the word that comes to my mind is *initiative*. Paul acknowledges that peace may not be possible. We don't control how other people respond. But Paul doesn't let us off the hook. Those seven words—*as far as it depends on you*—are about initiative. While you can't control how others respond, you are responsible for pursuing peace.

In her book *Fierce Conversations*, Susan Scott writes, "Our lives succeed or fail gradually, then suddenly, one conversation at a time. . . . The conversation is the relationship."[6]

Let those words soak in. *The conversation is the relationship.* Unless you learn how to have more honest conversations, you will have shallow relationships. Unless you learn to talk about the hard and uncomfortable stuff, your sense of community and team will be purely cosmetic.

Let me share with you some high-level principles to guide your thinking on this topic, and then the next chapter will get into the nuts and bolts of navigating an uncomfortable conversation.

Ignore the Small Offenses

Not every problem in an organization or team requires an uncomfortable conversation.

First Peter 4:8 says, "Above all, love each other deeply, because love covers over a multitude of sins."

Much of the time, the right thing for you to do is nothing. I know people can be annoying and frustrating. I get it. People often do the following:

- drop the ball
- don't follow through
- are moody

- say things they shouldn't
- are quirky
- show up late

- don't show up at all
- don't return your email
- throw you under the bus
- are controlling
- take too much credit
- talk too much
- have irritating habits
- get defensive

And that's all before noon on Monday! By the way, they could say the same about you. A healthy team environment needs a good dose of grace and people who opt to ignore the small offenses.

Choose to believe the best about your teammates, fill the gap with trust, and treat people the way you would want to be treated. I know when I have a bad day, I appreciate my teammates' extending a little extra grace.

Engage the Bigger Offenses and Conflicts

How do you know when you should have an uncomfortable conversation? I'm sure there are more, but I can think of at least five situations that require an uncomfortable conversation:

- When the situation is damaging your relationship with another person.
- When the other person's behavior is part of a destructive pattern.
- When the situation is negatively impacting the ministry or the team.
- When you have hurt or offended somebody. (Jesus was very clear about this. In Matthew 5:23–24, He says, "Therefore, if you are offering your gift at the altar and there remember that your brother or sister has something against you, leave your gift there in front of the altar. First go and be reconciled to them; then come and offer your gift.")
- When the person or situation is dishonoring God or the reputation of the body of Christ.

One reason I have such passion and conviction about this topic is because I haven't been very good at doing this through the years. Some of the biggest conflict and pain I have experienced in ministry (and caused others to experience) might have been avoided if I just would have been willing to have an uncomfortable conversation.

Here is the irony: in trying not to upset people and make waves, the opposite happens. In our attempt to avoid conflict, we end up creating more conflict.

There is no easy button when it comes to uncomfortable conversations. Having uncomfortable conversations is messy, but not having them ends up making things even more messy. A refusal to engage uncomfortable conversations ends up perpetuating dysfunction and spreading organizational disease.

Normalize Clear, Candid, and Kind Conversations

Each of us has a role to play in creating an environment where uncomfortable conversations can feel normal and safe. In other words, it is normal that when we have problems and conflicts, we sit down and talk about them. We are able to have calm, grown-up, reasonable, redemptive conversations. And no one is shamed or belittled when they appropriately address situations or relationships that are broken.

Before I get into the nuts and bolts of an uncomfortable conversation, let me give you a guiding principle. When it comes to conflict and problems, get into the habit of talking *to*, not talking *about* people. I have talked myself out of having an uncomfortable conversation with someone hundreds of times. You never want to rush into a hard conversation, but you don't want to run from it either. When something in your spirit nudges you to have the conversation, don't dismiss it. As Susan Scott says, "Don't just trust your instincts, obey them."[7]

An overwhelming majority of the time, when it comes to small offenses, irritations, or problems, the right thing to do is nothing. But every so often, a situation will arise where the right thing to do is have an uncomfortable conversation. You know it in your spirit, but everything in you recoils from the idea. Perhaps the most important step in any uncomfortable conversation is the first step. It is your willingness to sit down face-to-face and redemptively work through a hard situation.

Now, let me ask you a question. Is there something going on right now with a team member or somebody in your ministry that you are avoiding? Perhaps the situation causes you anxiety and stress every time you think about it. You brood over it. You rehearse the conversation in your head, but you can never seem to muster the courage to have the conversation in person. You know you need to address the issue, but you naïvely keep hoping it will just go away.

Don't keep walking around it day after day. Avoidance never really solves anything; it just prolongs the pain. Decide today to have the uncomfortable conversation.

TEAM DISCUSSION QUESTIONS

1. When you were growing up, how did your family handle conflict? How has this impacted how you handle conflict?

2. On the scale below, place an X on the line that would indicate your personal willingness to engage uncomfortable conversations.

Avoid like the plague ———————————————— Always take initiative to resolve

3. If you were coaching someone on how to have an uncomfortable conversation, what advice would you give them?

4. What could your team do better when it comes to having uncomfortable conversations?

25

How to Have an Uncomfortable Conversation

The numbers 28, 38, 53, 73, and 7 don't mean much by themselves. But they converged in an unbelievably tragic way in 1986. It was January 28 when the Challenger shuttle launched from the Kennedy Space Center. It was an unseasonably cold day in South Florida, a mere 38 degrees. In fact, a stretch of cold weather kept delaying the launch of the shuttle. The pressure was mounting to get on with the launch. Pressure was increasing, and patience was decreasing.

The problem was that the O-rings on the Challenger's fuel system had been designed for launch at temperatures of at least 53 degrees.

The night before the launch, Bob Ebeling and four other engineers at NASA contractor Morton Thiokol had tried to stop the launch. Their managers and NASA overruled them.

"NASA ruled the launch," he explains. "They had their mind set on going up and proving to the world they were right and they knew what they were doing. But they didn't."[1]

Only 73 seconds after launch, the Challenger exploded and all 7 astronauts lost their lives.

Bill Zipp writes the following about this dark day:

The greatest tragedy of this disaster was that it was entirely preventable. . . . I've read the transcripts of the actual conversations between NASA's leaders and the engineers at Morton Thiokol, designers of the space shuttle's fuel system, hours before the fateful decision to move forward was made. They sent shivers up my spine. The pages are filled with personal attack, angry accusations, and outright arrogance and animosity.

In short, the Challenger disaster was not an engineering failure, it was a failure in human relations.[2]

Churches and nonprofits blow up all the time because of unresolved conflict. We must learn how to resolve conflicts and find the courage to have uncomfortable conversations. Taking the initiative isn't enough; we must know *how* to engage these difficult conversations. By their very nature uncomfortable conversations are fraught with volatility and land mines.

In all honesty, I have a lot of uneasiness about writing this chapter. I want to get into the nuts and bolts of "how" you have an uncomfortable conversation. But there is no simple formula or three easy steps to having an uncomfortable conversation. Every situation is unique. The people involved are unique. The circumstances leading up to the conversation are unique. Uncomfortable conversations have so many nuances and variables that talking about the how can seem overly simplistic.

With that disclaimer, let me share with you some practical do's and don'ts of having an uncomfortable conversation. These practices have been birthed out of my experiences, but mostly they have emerged out of my mistakes. The steps I am going to mention are for the more serious issues that need to be addressed. You can always lessen the steps for a less weighty conflict or issue.

The first uncomfortable conversation is with yourself. You must make certain you are entering the conversation with the right motives and spirit. Until your motives are redemptive and sincerely seeking the best for the other person, you are not ready to have the conversation. And your spirit must be one of prayerful dependence.

James 1:5 says, "If any of you lacks wisdom, you should ask God, who gives generously." Because these situations are volatile, and because everyone is unique, you will need God's wisdom to effectively navigate them. The best soil for an uncomfortable conversation is one of prayer, humility, and love.

One of the most awkward aspects of an uncomfortable conversation is actually setting up the meeting. When you tell the other person you want to get together, they are obviously going to want to know the reason for the meeting, especially if they already sense a problem. Let me give you three pieces of advice about this.

1. Don't get into the uncomfortable conversation prematurely. In other words, don't have the conversation right then and there while you are simply trying to schedule the meeting.

2. Once you ask for the meeting, don't delay. Even if you need to rearrange schedules, make sure you have the meeting soon after scheduling it. The other person will be anxious and stressed, and it is unfair to them to delay the meeting.

3. Be honest but caring when you talk about the reason for getting together. Don't say things such as "It's not really a big deal" or "I just want to get together and chat." I prefer using statements such as "I have some concerns about _____ and I would like for us to talk about it together."

Be sure to find an appropriate place to meet where you can have privacy. And schedule plenty of time for the meeting. It is not unusual for an uncomfortable conversation to last longer than you expect. As a general rule, I try to have at least a half hour buffer in my schedule just in case the conversation goes longer than expected.

Once you have set up the meeting, you need to think about how you will get into the conversation. The first sixty seconds may be the most important. In my opinion, it is best to come straight at the issue and get to the point quickly. Don't engage in a lot of meaningless small talk. People can smell a hidden agenda a mile away.

Susan Scott says one of the errors we often make when having an uncomfortable conversation is that we use "too many pillows." We soften the message to lessen the impact and avoid hurting people's feelings. "The trouble is, sometimes we put so many pillows around a message that the message gets lost altogether."[3]

Personally, I think it is a good idea to write down ahead of time your opening sentence or two. Obviously, you aren't going to carry that paper into the meeting and read it to the other person. But writing down an opening sentence or two may help you articulate why you want to have the meeting and identify the core issue you want to address. Be clear, compassionate, and concise. Often, in my attempt to soften the blow, I meander around the core issue and as a result leave the person feeling confused. Your word choice matters. For a leader (especially in an uncomfortable conversation), no comment is insignificant. Sometimes as I have entered a hard conversation, I have been nervous and ended up stumbling over my words. Writing down what I want to say at the beginning of the conversation helps me be clear, even when I am nervous or way outside my comfort zone.

The old saying is true: "Thoughts disentangle themselves when they pass through the lips and the fingertips." If you can't write something down, it's not clear enough in your mind. Writing makes for clear and precise articulation.

If you have called the meeting, it is your job to lead it and not lose sight of the desired outcome. Susan Scott gives some great practical instruction for how we should start the meeting.

- Clearly name the issue/problem (from your perspective). Be clear and honest while at the same time doing your best to be respectful of the other person and what they may be feeling in that moment. Don't be shocked if they are surprised you are having this conversation.
- Clarify what is at stake. Is this an issue of friendship and relationship? Is this simply a course correction? Is their job on the line? If their job is on the line, hopefully you have already had other conversations addressing their performance.
- Articulate your desire and commitment to resolve the issue and to be redemptive. This is not about punishment or "being right." This is about resolving the issue and moving forward together.

- Own any contribution to the problem that is yours. Even if the issue is 98 percent them and just 2 percent you, you need to own your 2 percent.
- As you talk about the issues, watch your tone and choice of words. Don't make accusations. Be careful about expressing your assumptions as facts. And don't use a harsh tone. Your tone will set the tone of the meeting.
- Invite their response. Uncomfortable conversations should never be monologues. The word *conversation* implies that there is dialogue. This is not a session to vent all your pent-up frustrations. And when you invite their response, don't interrupt or become defensive.[4]

One mistake I have made in the past is assuming I have all the facts and deciding ahead of time how this conversation is going to play out.

I would strongly encourage you to be a curious listener when you are having an uncomfortable conversation. Ask good initial questions, then ask good follow-up questions. Truly listen to the other person's perspective. I have gone into a conversation thinking I had all the facts, but what I really had was just my interpretation of the facts. And what I quickly discovered is that there was another valid point of view that I needed to hear.

The word *confront* has a Spanish derivative, and the prefix "con" means "with." It means to be "with" someone. During an uncomfortable conversation, we are not to be "over" them or "out in front" of them, but "with" them.

This reflects a mind-set. Even though I might have called the meeting, and even though I might be taking the lead, I am inviting them into the conversation. In too many uncomfortable conversations, the outcome is a foregone conclusion.

Also, when you are in an uncomfortable conversation, don't talk too much. And don't be afraid of silence. When we are uncomfortable or unclear, our tendency is to ramble. Susan Scott says, "Of all the tools I use during conversations and all the principles I keep in mind, silence is the most powerful of all."[5]

198

How do you wrap up an uncomfortable conversation? Just as it is important to think through how to get into the conversation, it is important to know how to come out of the conversation.

Again, clarity must be a priority. If this is an uncomfortable conversation with a team member, you want clarity and resolution relationally and professionally. In other words, before the meeting is done, you want to make sure any relational issues have been resolved and anything that could be a divisive wedge in your relationship has been discussed and dealt with. If apologies, forgiveness, or reconciliation are necessary, they have been extended. The goal should always be mutual respect and love as brothers and sisters in Christ.

Often in an uncomfortable conversation there is a professional side to the discussion. Maybe what precipitated the conversation is the way the other person is impacting the morale or performance of the team. In that case, it is not enough to have relational harmony. Some next steps likely need to be taken after the conversation is done.

Before you wrap up the meeting, you must answer two critical questions.

1. *What has been decided?* This is about defining what resolution looks like. It is great to have a healthy conversation, but for the conversation to truly be helpful, there needs to be agreement about the decisions that have been made. Those decisions define what needs to change, so I like to articulate them in the meeting and make sure we both agree. Also, it is wise to write up a summary of the meeting afterward, specifically including decisions that were made. I suggest sending a copy of the summary to the other person.

2. *How do we move forward?* This is the game plan and next steps to solve the problem or issue that necessitated the hard conversation. I like the idea of asking the other person what next steps they think should be taken. In doing so, you are treating them like an adult, and they are more likely to own the action steps if they helped create them.

None of us come into the world with the ability to handle uncomfortable conversations well. It is a learned skill. In fact, it is counterintuitive to our fight-or-flight tendencies. But if you are in ministry leadership, it is a skill you must learn. In war, the worst kind of casualties are caused by friendly fire. You think you are part of a team fighting a common enemy, only to be taken out by your own teammate. The battlefields of ministry are littered with the casualties of friendly fire. I'm talking about the friendly fire of a dysfunctional team environment. I'm talking about the friendly fire of an insecure boss who doesn't know how to resolve conflict in a healthy way. I'm talking about the friendly fire of an organizational culture where the unspoken rule is "we just make nice."

We can do better. We *must* do better.

TEAM DISCUSSION QUESTIONS

1. The first uncomfortable conversation is with yourself. What would you say to yourself to prepare for an uncomfortable conversation?

2. What are some things you shouldn't do during an uncomfortable conversation?

3. If you were coaching someone on having an uncomfortable conversation, what one piece of counsel would you give them?

4. After you have had an uncomfortable conversation, what would you suggest as follow-up steps?

26

Inviting an Uncomfortable Conversation

Everything we've been talking about up to this point regarding uncomfortable conversations is child's play compared to what we are going to talk about now. This is the big leagues when it comes to challenging conversations.

In this chapter, I want to talk about inviting and receiving uncomfortable conversations. This is about being the kind of leader and team member who embraces honest feedback and even correction. This is about the person who is so committed to their personal growth that they are willing to walk through the stress and awkwardness of uncomfortable conversations. One way God matures and refines us is through conflict.

In the book of Proverbs, correction and rebuke are almost always seen as gifts.

Recently I was reading Proverbs 29, and in the first verse Solomon warns that "whoever stubbornly refuses to accept criticism will suddenly be destroyed beyond recovery" (NLT).

He's talking about our ability to receive an uncomfortable conversation.

The higher up you go in leadership, the more aggressively you will have to pursue this. The higher up in leadership you go, the more people are happy to put you on a pedestal and resist shooting straight with you. Over the years, I have worked with a number of people in ministry who have had to step down (at least temporarily) because of some kind of toxic behavior or sin or moral failure. One common thread in all these situations is relational isolation. There wasn't anybody who felt the freedom or permission to address the unhealthy behavior or pattern.

I remember working with a church where the pastor had been having an affair with another staff member. After the situation had blown wide open and become public, I had the chance to sit down with some of the staff. And each person I spoke with acknowledged that they had seen warning signs but had not had the courage to confront the situation.

You will likely have to go beyond passively giving permission to a friend to confront you. I suggest you find a person or two and tell them that if they see something in your life that isn't right, you don't just want them to feel permitted to confront you—you want them to feel a sense of responsibility. Our ability to self-deceive is incredibly powerful and has been the undoing of many people in ministry. Too much is at stake in your life and leadership to not have people speak honestly to you. I wonder how many pastors or leaders in ministry could have been saved from shipwrecking their lives if someone had just had the courage to speak the truth and have an uncomfortable conversation.

> The practice of discipline in the community of faith begins with friends who are close to one another. Words of admonition and reproach must be risked when a lapse from God's Word in doctrine or life endangers a community that lives together. . . . Nothing can be more cruel than leniency which abandons others to sin. Nothing can be more compassionate than that severe reprimand which calls another Christian in one's community back from the path of sin.[1]

Perhaps the biggest barrier to our inviting uncomfortable conversations is our own personal insecurity. So, let's just get this dirty little secret out in the open. Every single one of us is insecure. No one is exempt.

Even the most seemingly confident person on the team, who seems like they have it all together, is insecure. Accountability exposes and brings our insecurities to the surface. In my experience, our insecurities manifest themselves in two primary ways—defensiveness and defeat. Some people shut down while others blow up. Some react with self-condemnation and some with self-protection. But the underlying root of all the reactions is insecurity.

And because we are insecure, everything in us resists willingly inviting an uncomfortable conversation.

That's why doing the hard work in your interior life (soul) regarding your identity is so important. Only as you find your worth, value, and significance in your identity in Christ will you be in a position to invite an uncomfortable conversation. In the past when people would put the spotlight on my weakness, failure, or sin, I would be left internally devastated and filled with shame. But in recent years, as I have begun to rest in my identity in Christ, the grip of approval addiction has begun to loosen in my life.

It is still hard to be confronted. The voices of shame and inadequacy can still haunt me, but I am able to receive the honest feedback in a much healthier way—and there is great freedom in that.

When it comes to inviting uncomfortable conversations, my challenge to you is to lean in, not lean out. Tell your teammates you want to be held accountable and receive honest feedback. These moments are opportunities to grow and learn. This is a crucial part of our sanctification and spiritual formation. The reason some leaders have plateaued and been stuck for years is because of their unwillingness to let anyone get up close and personal. Their reluctance to reveal or talk about the stuff that is broken in them keeps them dangerously isolated.

By the way, not only is it healthy for us to invite uncomfortable conversations, but doing so models something very powerful for the team and helps create a culture of honest feedback.

I was asked to facilitate a retreat with a senior leadership team of a large church. The pastor let me know ahead of time that he wanted to develop a deeper level of trust among the team members. I shared with him that trust was best built within a culture of honor and honesty.

I also had the team do a little exercise I borrowed from Patrick Lencioni, and it was definitely uncomfortable. Each person in the room was singled out and every other person in the group had to answer two questions about them: (1) What does this person do that helps and contributes to the team? (2) What does this person do that hurts or hinders the team?

I wouldn't recommend doing this if your team hasn't been together for a little while. But the members of this group knew one another well. I explained the exercise and then said, "Let's start with the pastor. What's one thing he does to help or contribute to the team?" As you might expect, everyone was quick to offer their affirmation of this gifted leader. Then I asked, "What's one thing he does that hurts or hinders the team?" The room got deadly quiet. But with zero hesitation, the pastor physically leaned forward in his chair, looked at his team, and said, "Okay, guys, help me grow."

I don't know that I have ever been so proud of a pastor. I promise you that his stock skyrocketed with his team that day.

Now, sometimes when people show up in your life to have an uncomfortable conversation, their delivery can be quite poor. Sometimes they will poorly choose their words. Sometimes they will be abrasive and hurtful.

I once did a life plan for a pastor who had experienced an unbelievable tragedy in his family. He shared that one of the most difficult aspects of walking through that season was dealing with the inane and insensitive comments from people. He told me that his counselor had given him a piece of insightful advice that had been very helpful.

His counselor had said, "Don't listen to what people are actually saying; listen to what they're trying to say." When people have an uncomfortable conversation with you, their delivery, timing, and choice of words may be poor. But listen to what they are trying to say. What is the nugget of truth you need to hear?

Predecide that when someone feels the need to have an uncomfortable conversation with you, that you are going to be open and teachable.

In the first thirty seconds, you will set the tone of the conversation and expose how open you are to correction. I know it is hard, but resist the temptation to quickly jump in and explain or defend.

Listen. Wait. Be present.

My dear brothers and sisters, take note of this: Everyone should be quick to listen, slow to speak and slow to become angry. (James 1:19)

I have just one more piece of advice that has been very helpful in my own journey with uncomfortable conversations. No matter what the conflict is and what the person has pointed out, the truth is, I am far more messed up than they can imagine. Whatever they are putting their finger on, it is just the tip of the iceberg.

In his book *Surprised by Joy*, C. S. Lewis says he found inside himself "a zoo of lusts, a bedlam of ambitions, a nursery of fears, a harem of fondled hatreds."[2] Or as my friends in the South would say, "We are all a *hot mess.*"

There is a great story about a fourth-century monk named John the Short. I'm thinking about changing my name to Lance the Short. I digress. A jealous monk once approached John as he was teaching and said, "John, your cup is full of poison." John responded, "Yes . . . it is. But you said that when you could only see the outside; I wonder what you [would] say if you saw the inside."[3]

Here's the good news. You are more broken than you want to admit, but you are more blessed than you can imagine. When someone shines the spotlight on something ugly or broken in your life, or you mess up and feelings of insecurity begin to rise to the surface, *remember who you are in Jesus.*

He is not surprised by your weakness and brokenness, and it doesn't impact His unconditional love for you. That, my friend, is amazing.

You are a beloved child of God: redeemed, sanctified, made holy, declared righteous, adopted, accepted, loved, reconciled, chosen, justified, forgiven, blessed, saved, transformed, co-heir with Jesus, indwelt by the Spirit, on your way to heaven.

Here's the point. No conflict can shake your true identity. You are a child of the King. And next time someone brings an uncomfortable conversation to your doorstep, be like my pastor friend. Lean in. Look them in the eye. And say to them, "Okay, help me grow."

TEAM DISCUSSION QUESTIONS

1. What is the greatest personal barrier to your inviting uncomfortable conversations?

2. Who do you need to go to and give them not only the permission but also the responsibility to confront you if they see something ungodly in your life?

3. When someone confronts you or has an uncomfortable conversation with you, what is going on inside you while that is happening?

4. When someone challenges or confronts you, what is your typical initial response?

27

Handling a Hurricane

It is going to happen. Take it to the bank. You can count on it. It is inevitable. It is absolutely certain. As sure as the sun will come up in the morning, someone on your team or in your organization will have a disastrous moral failure. By the way, when I talk about moral failure, I'm not only referring to sexual sin. It could be related to finances or some other breach of ethical behavior.

We've seen it so much in recent years that it shouldn't surprise us any longer, but it still does. I think part of the reason we are surprised is because we are usually blindsided by it. We don't typically get any advance notice. Most often there isn't a gradual awareness. We are just rocking along, focusing on our ministry, and then *boom*. An unexpected hurricane hits and we never saw it coming. Such a storm will be devastating for the person involved and potentially for our church or organization.

Because we don't see what happens in secret, we can be lulled into a false sense of security that no one around us is in the midst of an impending disaster. But when the storm hits, it is a wake-up call. It is a sobering reminder that all of us are very human and very flawed. Every single one of us is catastrophically vulnerable to temptation and sin. And our power to self-deceive is incredibly strong. I am susceptible, and you are susceptible.

Don't be naïve or arrogant about what you are capable of. Spiritual warfare is real, and one of the most common battlegrounds is moral compromise.

If you know a disaster is headed your way, it is foolish and possibly disastrous not to prepare. On October 4, 2016, Matthew, a category 4 hurricane, pounded Haiti with 130 mph winds. Crawling at 8 mph, it then headed for Cuba and set its target for the southeast coast of the United States. While the hurricane was slamming Haiti, I saw news coverage of a popular beach in Florida. Everything looked normal. No wind, beautiful palm trees, majestic sunset, calm seas. But despite everything feeling normal on that Tuesday, everyone was diligently preparing for the disaster that was headed their way.

People were boarding up their windows, gassing up their cars, buying extra water and groceries, securing generators, and making sure their family had a safe place to ride out the storm.

After I left my position at Saddleback Church, I started doing some consulting with Christ Fellowship Church in the West Palm Beach area. One of the first days I was working with them, they dedicated an entire staff meeting to hurricane preparedness. They had a thorough plan in place and thought it was so important to be ready that they took the time to walk their staff members through the plan. They spent the first part of the meeting going over the game plan for boarding up and protecting the church facilities. Then they talked through how they would communicate once the hurricane hit. Their plan included organizing the staff for various responsibilities, communicating expectations of staff, and what they would do to help the community in the aftermath of a hurricane.

Honestly, for a kid from New Mexico who grew up in the desert, the plan was a little daunting and scary. But mostly it was impressive. They live in an area where hurricanes are a fact of life. And we live in a generation where moral failures among leaders are a fact of life. If we are wise, we will face the reality that moral failure will at some point impact our team. The hurricane is on the way—and we need to make the necessary preparations.

One way we prepare is to own our leadership responsibility when a hurricane hits. We each have a part to play and we don't get to outsource this. We don't get to leave town and let somebody else worry about the hurricane. No, we ride out the storm and then dig in to help with the cleanup.

The apostle Paul is very clear that we have a responsibility to deal appropriately with people in the church who fall into sin. And that would most certainly include someone who is on our team or in our ministry. Paul writes, "It isn't my responsibility to judge outsiders, but it certainly is your responsibility to judge those inside the church who are sinning" (1 Cor. 5:12 NLT).

That phrase—*it certainly is your responsibility to judge those inside the church who are sinning*—can make us more than a little uncomfortable. In this age of extreme tolerance, the thought of judging anyone makes us squirm. It is helpful to distinguish between judging and being judgmental. To be judgmental is to have an attitude of condemnation, contempt, and derision. To be judgmental is to look down our nose at someone. It is the feeling that we are "more than" and the other person is "less than."

That is very different from having to carry out the function of a judge. When I think of a judge, I think of someone who has been granted authority and whose job it is to uphold the law and hold people accountable.

The best judges carry out their duties without being judgmental.

Many of the young leaders on our teams have grown up in a time when we haven't talked much about these hard issues. Therefore, when the inevitable hurricane of moral failure hits a team, it often causes devastation, confusion, misunderstanding, and anger.

One way you can prepare your team for the hurricane is by teaching on this subject and discussing it together.

- What are the moral and character qualifications of spiritual leadership in the church?
- What does the Bible say about dealing with people who fall?
- What is the difference between how we treat someone as a person and how we deal with their position as a leader?
- How do we support those who are walking through a moral failure?
- How do we help them rebuild?

By the way, the worst time to teach on this is in the middle of the hurricane.

No matter how much teaching you do, and no matter how gently you deal with the person and the situation, you can expect people to think you are being harsh and condemning. In this age of tolerance, any kind of discipline or removal from leadership will be misunderstood. You will certainly have someone say, "I thought we were a place of grace."

Just like with an actual hurricane, no amount of preparation will eliminate the damage, but good preparation can minimize it. It is my hope that this chapter will help you and your team create a well-defined plan for dealing with a moral failure on your team.

By creating a plan, you are anticipating the moment you know is coming. There will be a day that feels like a normal day, except a hurricane is about to hit your team. If you have prepared, it won't be a "freak out" moment; it will be a "let's execute our hurricane plan" moment. Immediately after the hurricane has passed, the first step of action is to do a thorough assessment.

As a general rule, when the hurricane hits and you discover a team member has fallen, it is wise to put the person on a leave of absence for at least a few days so you can thoroughly assess. If they are an employee, I suggest a paid leave of absence. In the midst of these painful situations, look for opportunities to be gracious. Putting someone on a paid leave of absence is gracious and demonstrates care for the person involved. By putting them on a leave of absence, you effectively release the pressure valve, giving you time to figure out how you need to handle the situation.

These types of situations can feel extremely urgent, but a little breathing room and a little patience can be a great help. One reason this is true is the fact that you never have the whole story at the beginning. There are always layers to the story that you uncover only as you begin to dig into the situation. And my forty years of leading teams has taught me that these situations are always worse than I thought they were when they first came to light. Never once have I started to dig into a situation and been pleasantly surprised that it wasn't as bad as I had originally thought.

While it is helpful to have enough time to discover the truth about the entire situation, you don't want to let situations like these linger very long. When you are dealing with a hurricane, it is not business as usual. You put other demands on hold so you can give adequate time and focus to the crisis.

And, just like when a hurricane hits, there is no way to anticipate everything. No matter how thorough your plan is, you will discover intricacies and nuances that you couldn't have predicted. Just know going in that there will be things you didn't plan for. There is no simple formula for handling a moral failure on your team.

I think it is helpful to acknowledge your desire to handle the situation prayerfully, carefully, gracefully, and clearly—but you won't handle it perfectly. The one thing you can count on is that the situation will be messy. And it will require courage for you to lead well through the crisis.

Having a plan and predeciding (as much as you can) your actions will help you handle these situations objectively rather than emotionally. I also encourage you to be clear about what you believe the Bible teaches about handling a moral crisis in the life of a ministry leader. When you are being scrutinized and criticized, your conviction serves as an anchor that you are doing what is right and biblical. In these moments, you must care more about what God thinks than what others think.

When the situation comes to light, give yourself adequate time to fully discover the truth of the situation—don't overreact or make an impulsive decision. Have candid but grace-filled conversations with those involved. Seek counsel only from a handful of advisors who are mature, wise, experienced, and can hold the situation in confidence. Then, once you have had conversations with those involved and prayed and sought good counsel, make a clear and definitive decision as to what you will do in this situation.

Communicate frequently and clearly with the people involved. Don't leave them to wonder. Minutes will feel like hours and hours will feel like days to them. And most of all, don't let them hear updates or new information second- and thirdhand.

Paul is clear in Galatians 6 regarding the heart and spirit of how we engage the hurricane. He writes, "Brothers and sisters, if someone is caught in a sin, you who live by the Spirit should restore that person gently. But watch yourselves, or you also may be tempted" (Gal. 6:1). We need to approach the situation with a broken heart and a spirit of gentleness.

But just as it is important to be gentle, it is equally important to be clear. Here's the problem for most of us. Those of us who lead in ministry organizations are usually diplomatic and polite. Having difficult conversations is tough for us. We work hard not to hurt people. Most of the time this style of communication serves us well. But when dealing with a crisis on the team, we have to communicate differently.

Here is my challenge to you: don't let your diplomacy lead to a lack of clarity. Being unclear is being unkind.

Often in a moral crisis, the decision needs to be made that the person step down from their role—at least temporarily, if not permanently. I used to think this was primarily about discipline for their sin. And while discipline is a factor, over the years I have come to see this as "severe mercy." The person will almost never see it as an act of mercy, but I believe it gives them time and space to rebuild. And in the end, that can be a real gift.

And while it might be necessary for them to step aside from their position, they don't need to step aside from relationships and community. It is easy for the person to feel very isolated. Authentic care and friendship are two of the most critical components in the process of healthy restoration. If someone on your team or in your ministry organization has a moral failure, decide right now that you will love and care for them, not cast them aside. The old saying "Out of sight, out of mind" is very relevant to this topic. Once the person isn't around the office or in meetings, it is easy to just move on, inadvertently making the person feel isolated and judged. One of the greatest gifts you can give someone who is walking through a moral failure is to reach out and simply be a caring friend.

Also, as part of your hurricane crisis plan, it is imperative that you be able to separate your love for them as a person from the decision you have to make about them as a leader. The reason the Bible gives us qualifications for leadership is that leaders are held to a higher standard. Extending grace and love and forgiveness to a person is a given. That is our biblical mandate. But that is different from being qualified (at least for now) to carry out a leadership role.

As Rick Warren says, "Forgiveness is a personal issue but trust is a positional issue. Forgiveness is instant. But trust is a different issue. Trust is rebuilt slowly and trust is not built on grace. Trust is built on behavior."[1] The foundation on which trust is rebuilt is credibility. With a moral failure comes a loss (temporarily) of credibility. And it will take some time to rebuild credibility and trust.

Once you have worked through the situation and made a clear decision about the consequences, you now have to carefully think through the communication.

Don't sweep the situation under the rug or pretend the crisis didn't happen. You can be assured that the story will leak out. In a communication vacuum, people will make up things worse than the truth. But your communication must be carefully crafted. And in our litigious culture, you must consider legal ramifications. I have found it helpful to seek good counsel on what to communicate and to write out exactly what I plan to communicate. This is an area where you cannot shoot from the hip, and being sloppy in your communication will make the hurricane worse.

An obvious question is, "Who needs to know?" My general rule of thumb is to share as broadly as their role and influence in the church. If the person is a children's worker, there's no need to share their moral failing with the whole church. However, if it is the lead pastor, the entire congregation deserves to know what is going on. As part of the communication, I have found it helpful to ask people not to pursue details or gossip. People's lives and families are affected.

Another thing I settled early on in dealing with these situations is that you do not owe it to people in your church or ministry to answer all their questions or share all the information. This has created some very uncomfortable moments as people have pressed and even demanded to know the specifics. I have kindly but directly let them know a leadership structure is in place to deal with the issue, and they are carefully and prayerfully handling the situation.

You will be criticized no matter how you handle such circumstances. In protecting the person who created the hurricane and the details of the situation, you will often take the brunt of criticism. Just expect it. It comes with the territory. Even though you didn't create the situation, you can become the lightning rod for it. Personally, my knee-jerk reaction to such criticism is to become defensive and protect myself. But this is a test of my maturity as a leader. It is an opportunity for me to lead with graciousness and do what is best for the organization and the people involved—even if that means being misunderstood and falsely accused.

Finally, when possible, work with the person to create a restoration plan. That doesn't necessarily mean restoration to their former role, but restoration of their soul and life and relationships. When a hurricane sweeps through a community, you don't just clean up the debris. You rebuild. And it is always a wonderful sight to see a structure rebuilt that is more beautiful and stronger than what was destroyed. It doesn't happen very often in the church or ministry organizations, but when it does, it is a beautiful thing.

TEAM DISCUSSION QUESTIONS

1. How does it make you feel when Paul says it is our responsibility to judge those inside the church who are sinning?

2. When someone has a moral failure, how is asking them to step down from their position a "severe mercy"?

3. How can you love and support people who are walking through a moral failure?

4. What is something you should avoid doing or saying when someone is walking through a moral failure?

28

Transition Isn't
a Four-Letter Word

One reality of team life is that people will occasionally choose to transition off your team. It is my experience that leaving a church or parachurch ministry feels different from leaving a secular business. It feels more emotionally charged. For a variety of reasons, when a person chooses to leave a team and join another team, people in the world of ministry tend to take it more personally. There can be a sense of hurt, abandonment, or even betrayal. The result is that people in ministry often don't feel safe to tell anyone they are considering a move.

But people begin to consider transitioning off a team for many different reasons:

- a restlessness in their spirit
- their gifts aren't a good match for their position
- a prompting from the Holy Spirit
- dysfunction in the organization's culture
- personal and family reasons
- conflict with their supervisor

- a seemingly better opportunity
- they aren't succeeding in their role

They secretly begin to pursue a role on another team and go through the interview process under the cover of night. That's exactly how I approached transition early in my ministry. It's all I knew and the only thing I had ever seen modeled. The process always felt sneaky, underhanded, and deceitful. The truth is, it felt wrong. While the process itself felt sketchy, the end result was even more brutal.

Suppose you become aware of an opportunity that intrigues you, so you send your resume from a private email account. That is followed by a series of phone calls and information gathering with the potential church or organization. If they are still interested in you, they invite you for an on-site visit and interview. You sneak away for a couple days and try to navigate the trip in such a way that no one at your current church knows you are flirting with another church.

While you are on this "secret" visit, you are always nervous that somebody back home is going to catch wind of what is going on. If the on-site visit goes well, the church or organization will then extend an official offer for you to take the position.

This is a moment of extreme internal conflict. On the one hand, you are excited about the new opportunity and all the potential that comes with it. On the other hand, you know you have to go back and face the music. You now have to let your team and congregation (who up to this point have been completely in the dark) know you are leaving. Having walked through this experience a couple of times, let me tell you from firsthand experience that it is gut-wrenching.

I want to go on record and say that this approach to transition *stinks*. It creates huge stress, fractures relationships, and perpetuates a dysfunctional system. It needs to be ceremoniously thrown in the dumpster. There is a better way.

In the rest of this chapter and the next, I want to share with you what I believe is a better way.

For there to be any chance of our really doing this in a healthier way, we must consider two angles. First, we must talk about how we as leaders create an environment that is conducive to healthy transition. Second, we must talk about how we as individuals handle the process when we are considering leaving the team.

It is imperative for team members and team leaders to acknowledge how significant transitions are in shaping team and organizational culture. How you handle the process of transition says a lot about how you treat people, how you celebrate people, how you handle hard things, how you communicate, and how kingdom-minded you are.

Leading the Transition Process

Let's be honest. If you care about your vision and you care about your team, losing good people is painful and hard. These are people you have loved, invested in, prayed with, and done ministry with. But as Henry Cloud says, "There is a big difference between hurt and harm."[1] It does hurt to lose good people, but we can do it in a way that doesn't harm the person, the team, the culture, or the organization. To do this well requires you to be unselfish and mature.

Have a transition mind-set.

Life is filled with transitions, for both you and those you love. It is normal and healthy for your kids to grow up and transition out of your house. It is normal to transition from being single to being married. It is normal to transition from college life to career life. And it is normal for God to transition people from one assignment to another. One of the most significant perspective shifts you can make is to normalize transition.

Henry Cloud says, "If you see them [endings] as normal, expected, and even a good thing, you will embrace them and take action to execute them. You will see them as a painful gift."[2]

Transitions are pathways to growth: for you as a leader, for the person leaving, for the organization, and for the person who will eventually fill the open position. The position's vacancy will become somebody else's opportunity. The person's leaving is actually part of the development path for somebody else.

In the moment, though, as a leader, what you feel is the loss. You feel the loss of the relationship, the loss to the team, and the loss of productivity. And you also feel the stress of having to go through the process of filling the vacancy. You feel the pressure of someone else having to pick up the load the transitioning person was carrying. But if you can accept that transition is normal, it will help you handle that sense of loss in a much healthier way.

Create an "open" environment.

To have a truly open environment, there has to be a kingdom mind-set. You must be able to see beyond "my" church or "my" organization. If every time a pastor or staff member or volunteer leaves, you feel as though they are betraying you or stabbing you in the back, you will foster an environment where people will handle transition in the dark.

It would be so much healthier to create an environment that communicates something like this: "When you are beginning to question whether it is time to leave, it's okay and safe to come early on in the process and have an honest conversation about your possible transition." I know this is the point when some of you are thinking to yourselves, *What have you been smoking? There isn't a chance that could happen here.* I am fully aware that in many organizations and churches, the moment you mention a possible transition, at best you are marginalized and at worst you are invited off the team.

An open environment can only be created in a culture where people know that your first priority is not what you want *from* them, but what you want *for* them. And if transitioning off the team is best for them and for the kingdom, then you can authentically bless and celebrate that. Sometimes you might not think their transition is best for them or the kingdom, but at the end of the day it is their decision, and even if you disagree with their decision, you can graciously release them.

By the way, it is not enough to just say that this is a safe place. If you don't model and demonstrate it, people won't take the risk. And if your culture has not been a safe place to talk about possible transition, then you need to be realistic and realize that it is going to take awhile to reshape the culture.

One thing I love about a safe and open environment is that it allows you to pray for and journey with this staff member as they consider a possible move. As a leader, it is difficult not to put your ministry and vision first. But sometimes the right thing to do is take off your leader hat and put on your shepherd hat.

The truth is, no matter how diligently you work to create an open environment, some people will still choose to transition in the dark. But it is still best to create a safe environment where there can be honest and grace-filled dialogue.

Lead decisively.

If you are the leader of the team or organization, once you have walked with this person and they have made the decision to transition, you must now put on your leader hat. I am not a fan of letting them linger too long in their current role. I want to work with the person leaving to figure out the best timeline for their transition. And while I want to include them in the dialogue, I must take the lead. There are no hard and fast rules about this (and there are some valid exceptions), but two to four weeks is a good transition period once the decision has been made. Once a person has decided to leave, their heart and attention will naturally begin to turn toward their new assignment.

Two to four weeks allows them enough time to wrap up their current work and bring relational closure. I also encourage you to make it a high priority for that person to document all the processes they utilize in their role. Consider doing an exit interview. They have a unique perspective, and you want to get their candid assessment.

It is a good idea to communicate to that person that you don't want them starting anything new or making any changes to the ministry before they leave. Let them know you are counting on them to finish well. Encourage them to be faithful and diligent and honoring of the church or organization until they walk out the door on their last day.

Carefully think through the communication.

Don't underestimate the importance of careful communication. Think through what you will communicate and the timeline for communicating.

The higher profile the position, the weightier the communication becomes. Words matter. Have a thorough plan, because if you don't, it can (and probably will) come back to bite you. Sit down with the person leaving and develop a communication plan together. Once the word is out, it spreads rapidly through the grapevine.

When thinking about the communication, two words can help guide you: *honest* and *honorable*. Make a commitment that when you are leading a staff transition, you will not "spin" the communication. Michael Abrashoff, author of *It's Your Ship*, writes, "Your people are more perceptive than you give them credit for, and they always know the score—even when you don't want them to."[3]

I promise you, when you spin the communication, your team can smell it a mile away. And when that happens, you undermine your own credibility as a leader. You may not share a lot about this person's transition. But make sure that whatever you do share is honest.

And then be honorable. Treat them with dignity and honor them for their contribution. Your team will be carefully listening to what you say and don't say. And they will be watching to see how you treat people on the way out. That will inform how they will approach a possible transition.

I also encourage you to clearly share your expectations with the person leaving. Who can they communicate with? When should they talk to them? And what would be appropriate and not appropriate to share with others?

Celebrate appropriately.

Before we talk about celebrating the person, I want you to know it is good and healthy to acknowledge sadness and a sense of loss when a team member transitions.

But you also want to celebrate them. This helps shape a healthy culture. Do a good job of honoring and celebrating them. Make it special. This communicates volumes to the church and staff. Also, use this as a teachable moment to talk about a kingdom mind-set. But whatever their position, bless them, affirm them, and honor them.

If we can begin to do this better, the by-product will be that we create a healthier team culture and fewer people will actually desire to leave the team.

Just this week I received an email from someone who worked on my team more than a decade ago. It was one of the most meaningful notes I have received in many years. He and I would both agree that the entire time we served together, our work relationship felt hard and more than a little strained. When he transitioned off the team, even though it removed the strain, I hated that we separated on less than great terms. But I think we both did our best to be honest and honorable in walking through his transition. In his email to me, he shared, "I did feel like you cared and were always available to me. I am grateful for the time I had working with you. You were always so patient with me and my rebellious spirit."

His words make me sound better than I was, and time has airbrushed some of my inadequacies. His email was a powerful reminder to me that transitions are hard, but when we are gracious and honoring, in His timing, God will honor us.

TEAM DISCUSSION QUESTIONS

1. What is the best organizational transition you have been through? What made it good?

2. In your opinion, what would be a healthy way for your organization to approach transition?

3. What are some of the negative consequences for a church's or organization's culture when you "spin" communication?

4. What could your organization do to appropriately celebrate the person who has decided to leave?

29

How to Transition Honestly and Honorably

The dictionary defines *transition* as "the process or a period of changing from one state or condition to another."[1] Changing from one state to another is not about moving from Georgia to Arizona. I like to think of transition as the land of "in-between."

The people of Israel had a long in-between transition going from Egypt to the promised land. What was true for the Israelites has also been true of the ministry transitions I have made during my life:

- They always include unexpected twists and turns.
- They are an uncomfortable time of growth and development.
- They are longer and messier than expected.
- They are filled with a sense of both loss and hope.
- God is faithful.

A word that I believe best describes transition is *disequilibrium*. When you experience disequilibrium, you lose your balance and stability. It is unnerving and uncomfortable.

I'm sure as you have walked through various life transitions, disequilibrium has been part of the journey. The question I want to try to answer in this chapter is, "How do you navigate the land of in-between?" In other words, if you are beginning to sense that your time is up in your current ministry, how do you leave well?

My observation is that those of us in the ministry world do not have a great track record when it comes to healthy transitions. It seems as though we don't talk about it much until we are already in it. Also, as a general rule, most leaders haven't spent time coaching their teams about how to approach a possible transition. If we have seen transitions go poorly with other people on the team, it can make a possible transition seem even more risky and fraught with land mines.

I realize you don't control certain things in your church or organization. But what you do control is how you walk through the land of in-between. Let me share with you some practical principles that might be helpful when you have to navigate a transition.

Seek God

I don't offer the direction to seek God as a spiritual platitude. Too often in my life I have evaluated opportunities based on the seeming merit of the opportunity. Was it a position of increased influence? Was it a bigger platform? Was it a more desirable position? Would I get paid more? Was it in a more desirable location to live? Would it be good for my family?

Spiritual discernment moves beyond intellectually and emotionally evaluating options and opportunities. It moves beyond simply listing the pros and cons. Discernment puts us in a place of listening and responding to the voice of the Spirit.

Ruth Haley Barton challenges us to pray what she calls a "Prayer of Indifference." It is modeled after the words of Jesus when He prayed, "Not my will but yours be done." She writes, "In the context of spiritual discernment, indifference is a positive term signifying that I am indifferent to anything but God's will. This is interior freedom or a state of openness to God in which we are free from undue attachment to any particular outcome. . . .

We ask God to bring us to a place where we want God's will, nothing more, nothing less, nothing else."[2]

Some questions we need to ask are: What are my motives for considering a transition? Am I running from something? Am I looking for an escape simply because I am in a hard situation? Am I looking for my significance in a different position?

I don't know about you, but discerning my motives always feels challenging. Rarely do I feel that all my motives are noble, and rarely do I feel that none of my motives are noble. Most of us walk around with a mixed bag of God motives and self motives. That's why it is important to submit our hearts and motives before the Lord.

> All a person's ways seem pure to them,
> but motives are weighed by the LORD. (Prov. 16:2)

> A person may think their own ways are right,
> but the LORD weighs the heart. (Prov. 21:2)

Seek God in Community

The truth is, when it comes to considering other opportunities, we see what we want to see. We often get in the way of making decisions about our own lives. Our past scripts, warped self-talk, daunting failures, paralyzing fears, and compelling voices make it hard to get clarity. We intuitively know we need the help of others to properly discern direction in our lives. Yet that can feel risky.

That is the beauty of the body of Christ. God has given you relationships and friendships with people who can have a more objective perspective. I know it might feel risky, but I believe you should involve the person or persons in authority over you early on in considering a transition. Often, in the world of ministry, they are the last people you talk to rather than one of the first.

It would be awesome to invite a few people whom you work closely with to help you discern a possible transition. It provides you the opportunity to get their objective appraisal, seek their help in evaluating how well the new position might fit your gifting, and invite them to join you in prayer.

I have been involved in situations where someone sought out a new position in a different ministry and never talked to anybody in their current ministry until they had already accepted the position. And on more than one occasion I have had the leader say, "If I would have known they were considering leaving, I would have sat down with them to see if we could figure out a way that they could stay."

By talking early on with those in authority over you, if and when you do transition, no one is caught off guard. They have had time to be in the discernment process rather than simply be informed of the decision.

Someone has said regarding transitions: "You want to leave in such a way that the back door is left open and the porch light is on." In other words, you want to still have good relationships and be welcomed in the place you are leaving.

Expect Your Emotional Health to Be Revealed

Part of the disequilibrium that you feel in a transition has to do with your own emotional health journey. Transitions turn up the heat on issues of identity, significance, differentiation, and loss:

- Is my identity truly anchored in Jesus, or is it found in my ministry role?
- Is my sense of significance rooted in what I accomplish in ministry or in the reality that I am a child of God?
- Do I have enough differentiation that I can be at peace even if people are disappointed in me for leaving?
- Do I know how to appropriately grieve and experience loss as I transition?

When you are journeying through a transition, the level of your emotional health will be exposed. As you journey in the land of "in-between," pay attention to your emotions and the questions above.

Submit to Leadership

If you have discerned that it is indeed time to leave, make a commitment to do what is best for the ministry you are leaving, not just the one you are going to. It is not wrong to leave, but it is wrong to leave poorly. How you leave your ministry role will reveal a lot about your heart for Jesus and His bride. Part of what will ensure that you leave well is to submit to those in leadership over the ministry.

Ask those in leadership, "How can I leave in a way that is best for this ministry?" As much as possible, submit to your current leaders as you determine the timeline, communication, handoff of responsibilities, and so on.

One of the most important areas for you to dialogue with your leaders about is the communication plan. You must think through how your leaving will be relayed to the people who should be informed about your transition. Being careless with communication always creates misunderstanding and hard feelings. Take the time to thoughtfully craft a communication plan by asking the following questions:

- What is the communication timeline?
- What will you and the leaders say about your leaving, and what won't you say?
- Who will you tell in person, and when will you tell them?
- What communication will there be to those in your ministry area?

Even if there has been conflict or you haven't been led well or the culture is dysfunctional, you have a responsibility to protect the unity of the body and reputation of Jesus. I am not saying you should be disingenuous, but you must guard against doing or saying anything that would undermine the work of God in the ministry you are leaving.

Don't Have a Long Funeral

Again, I would suggest working out the timeline with those in authority over you, but as a general rule, once you have made the decision to leave, don't linger very long. As I said in the last chapter, two to four weeks gives you enough time to wrap up your current responsibilities, make the handoff to whomever is going to cover your workload, and have relational closure with those on the team.

Also, don't take it personally, but people will quickly move on with their lives. For you, this is a major life-changing moment. But for the rest of the team, it is simply another transition. When I have left ministry positions in the past, it has been like pulling your fist out of a bucket of water. The hole is quickly covered and things quickly return to normal. The truth is, we are all expendable, and for all the people around us, life will return to normal as soon as we leave. That doesn't mean they don't love us and we won't be missed, but don't expect there to be weeping and gnashing of teeth.

Leave Your Place of Ministry Better than You Found It

Just follow this principle—leave it better than you found it—and your transition will go well. In the final weeks before your departure, work as though you are not leaving. Show up on time, be present in your meetings, follow through, and have a strong work ethic. When Paul was talking to slaves about how they were to conduct themselves, he said, "Work with enthusiasm, as though you were working for the Lord rather than for people" (Eph. 6:7 NLT). I think *enthusiasm* is a good word for how to carry out your ministry even when you are about to leave.

However, as you work hard right up until the last hour, don't start new things or make changes on your way out. In the days of your transition, your job is to stabilize and organize. Any time someone leaves, it raises questions. And part of your job is to be a stabilizing presence. The other part of your job is to organize your role so that it will be easier for someone to step in and take over your responsibilities. That means documenting processes and tying up loose ends.

Get Out of the Way

As a general rule, once the word is out that you are leaving, I would advise against sitting in meetings about the future of the ministry. Since you won't be there, it's just awkward for you to participate in discussions about the future. I am not advocating blowing off meetings, but I am suggesting working with your supervisor to decide what meetings you need to attend.

As I close this chapter, I want you to picture in your mind a "moment." You have prayerfully discerned that it is time to leave your current ministry role. You have met with those in leadership and together crafted a communication plan. You have diligently tried to make the handoff easy for the person who will take your position. You are appropriately grieving the loss of what you are leaving, but you are also anticipating what God has in the future.

It is now your last day. You have turned in your keys, handed back your computer, and cleaned out your workspace. As you walk out the door to your new assignment, you feel a profound sense of gratitude. You didn't handle everything perfectly, but you did your best to do this transition in an honest and honorable way. And as the door closes behind you, you feel the smile of your heavenly Father. You have finished well and successfully navigated the land of in-between.

My hope is that when you have to walk through your next transition, you will have that moment.

TEAM DISCUSSION QUESTIONS

1. When thinking about a transition, what does spiritual discernment in community look like?
2. If you were to consider a transition, how would you handle it with your current boss and organization?
3. In your opinion, what should people *not* do while walking through a transition?
4. Practically speaking, when going through a transition, what things should people do so that they finish well?

PART 7

CRAFT THE CULTURE

What do Chick-fil-A, Southwest Airlines, and Ritz-Carlton all have in common? All three of these exceptional organizations have an intentional and well-defined culture. Their team culture sets them apart. In this section, we will examine ways to build a life-giving, healthy, and high-performing culture.

30

Defining Organizational DNA

According to Merriam-Webster, the most popular word of 2014 was *culture*. "It's already a popular word, but culture has had a surge in interest this year because it can mean so many things."[1]

Culture is one of those words that is hard to define but easy to feel. You feel it every time you stay in a foreign country. You feel it every time you visit a church that is not your flavor. And when it comes to organizational health and effectiveness, while it may be hard to define, you can't overestimate the importance of culture. Sam Chand, in his book on church culture, writes, "Culture—not vision or strategy—is the most powerful factor in any organization."[2] In one survey, 95 percent of job candidates believe culture is more important than compensation.[3]

Tony Hsieh is the CEO of Zappos, a company that has become the poster child for building culture. Tony says, "Our number one priority is company culture. Our whole belief is that if you get the culture right, most of the other stuff like delivering great customer service or building a long-term enduring brand will just happen naturally on its own."[4]

Culture: Every Organization Has One

When you encounter a great organizational culture, it is a beautiful thing to experience and behold.

I recently read a story about a guy who visited Dave Ramsey's organization called The Lampo Group. Let me quote a couple of sentences about his experience: "Every team member I encountered (and I mean every team member) demonstrated passion, a positive attitude and outstanding customer service. . . . When we toured the organization's building, we received nothing but a warm reception, homemade sweets at the café, and a positive attitude from each staff member we met."[5] Wow! What he was describing was his encounter with culture. And that doesn't happen by accident. No organization ever just wandered into a great culture.

The Lampo Group's culture sets the company apart. In churches, doctrine or music or community focus or style of preaching can be a differentiator, but culture is also huge.

KFC and Chick-fil-A both sell chicken, but they have radically different cultures. Over-the-top friendliness and exceptional customer service has been a key differentiator for Chick-fil-A. Southwest Airlines flies commercial planes just like every other airline. But in a day when airlines have struggled to make a profit, Southwest has become one of the most profitable airlines in aviation history. And it largely has to do with culture.

If you ask me what words come to mind when I think about the way Southwest does business, I think of *fun, casual, friendly, helpful,* and *humorous.* In an industry that is always dealing with stressed-out and frustrated people, that kind of culture is a huge differentiator.

One church I work with, Christ Fellowship, in the West Palm Beach area, puts a high value on hospitality. Every church I know would declare that they put a high value on people. But one behavior that differentiates Christ Fellowship from many other churches is their gracious and thoughtful treatment of people. When you drive onto the campus, you will see a big sign that says "Welcome Home," and the people at Christ Fellowship work hard at what they call the "Welcome Home" experience. The senior leaders highly value hospitality, and it is now part of the culture of the entire organization. It isn't something they just talk about and put on a poster; it shows up in the behaviors of the team.

We all want to work in a healthy culture, but actually creating a culture that acts and behaves in healthy ways is easier said than done. That shouldn't surprise us. Think about your own ministry environment. Everyone who joins your team (including you) shows up with a backpack full of assumptions, experiences, expectations, and insecurities. On top of that, every single one of us is imperfect, flawed, and sinful. Building a team that is aligned, empowered, collaborative, trusting, hardworking, passionate, open, authentic, and productive is no small task.

Culture is one of those things that when it is good, it is really good. And when it is bad, it can be really bad—even toxic and damaging. A healthy culture will turbocharge your vision. An unhealthy culture will erode vision and derail strategy. According to a famous quote attributed to Peter Drucker, "Culture eats strategy for breakfast." Or as Sam Chand says, "Toxic culture is like carbon monoxide: you don't see it or smell it, but you wake up dead."[6]

If culture is that important, why don't more ministries put significant energy into creating and building the culture they desire? In my mind, there are at least two significant reasons. First, culture rarely feels urgent. But next Sunday's services or the donor dinner or the student camp coming up this month—those always feel urgent. They have a ticking clock attached to them. No one on your team has ever said, "We only have until the twenty-fifth to get the culture built." Second, most leaders are so focused on what they are trying to accomplish that they don't see how much the team culture impacts the desired results. What catapulted Toyota to being a world-class car manufacturer was that they focused not only on building cars but also on the culture of the team building the cars. They saw clearly the connection between culture and results.

Every church and ministry organization has a distinct culture, a unique DNA that makes them who they are. But most often that culture isn't articulated or evaluated. In many organizations, the culture is unspoken and unexamined. The best companies and ministries are very intentional in their focus on culture.

It has been said that culture is the unspoken rules of how things get done. Once you have been an insider for a while, you figure out how things get done in your ministry. You understand how decisions are made, you understand the quirks of the senior leader, you understand how conflict is dealt with, you understand how meetings are done, and you quickly come to understand what things you shouldn't say in a meeting. Whether or not the culture is dysfunctional, once you have been in the organization for a while, it becomes normal for you. It's sort of like a fish in a river; he doesn't notice the water. It completely surrounds him and is just the environment he swims in.

For team health and effectiveness (and for the sake of new people joining the team), someone must speak the unspoken rules. The team culture of most ministry organizations I have been around is squishy and loaded with land mines.

What Is Culture?

What is culture? If you had to define culture in fifteen seconds, what would you say? Not easy, is it? When it comes to culture, you feel it before you can describe it. You experience it before you can explain it. You certainly notice it when you visit a foreign country and bump up against different customs and ways of doing things, but you also encounter it when you enter a business, church, or organization.

There is a certain style or personality of an organization that is an expression of culture. I sometimes think of culture as the organization's way of doing what they do. There is a Ritz-Carlton way of doing customer service. There is a Starbucks way of doing business. There is a Salvation Army way of doing ministry.

Culture is the collective personality of an organization, composed of assumptions, beliefs, traditions, values, and attitudes. Ideally, these cultural qualities drive and govern desired behaviors.

Culture never stays at the level of the theoretical. It always manifests itself in behavior. In some ministry organizations, the cultural assumption is that we don't deal with conflict head-on. The resulting behaviors are things such as gossip; talking about people, not to people; and avoiding tension in meetings.

"The culture of a company is the behavior of its leaders. Leaders get the behavior they exhibit and tolerate."[7]

As Aristotle said, "We are what we repeatedly do."

I know some of you are reading this chapter and wondering if all this culture talk actually helps the team move forward in executing your ministry's vision. Or is this about creating a warm-fuzzy, feel-good environment where everyone can sit around a campfire singing "Kumbaya"?

Culture is not just a way to make people feel good about where they work. This entire chapter is built on the belief that constructing a healthy culture is not only right but also effective and productive. When people feel valued, they work harder. When there is less office politics, there will be less sideways energy diverted to deal with dysfunction. When there is higher collaboration, there is more buy-in. When there is authenticity and humility from leadership, there is more respect and less turnover. Culture and results are inseparably linked. Dave Ridley, who served as chief marketing officer for Southwest, said, "At Southwest we believe profitability and culture go hand in hand."[8]

I think of culture like gasoline and your ministry like an engine. It's not enough to have high-quality gasoline. No one ever holds up a gallon of fuel and says, "Wow, what great-looking gasoline that is." *No.* Gasoline is purposeful. It is for powering the engine. High-octane gas and a powerful engine will get traction quickly. But a high-powered engine (ministry) with polluted gas (culture) will cause the engine to sputter.

In a Christ-centered organization, the leader of a team and the entire organization must have a dual focus. First, they must focus on creating a culture that facilitates progress toward the vision. Second, they must focus on creating a culture that is healthy and life-giving for those on their team. A good question for all leaders to ask is, For the people who work in our organization, is the culture transforming or deforming?

The people who have worked with your ministry for the last five years should be better people and have better lives because of their time with your organization. One of the best indicators of this is whether people would recommend that their friends work there.

As I finish this chapter today, I am sitting in one of my favorite little coffee shops in the mountains of Colorado. I'm not sure what the coffee shop's mission statement is. I don't know what their strategic plan is. Their building isn't the greatest and their parking is pretty lousy, but I absolutely know what their culture is—casual, warm, friendly, rustic, and personal.

Their product isn't just their coffee and pastries (the what). Lots of places sell coffee and pastries. Their product is also the environment and culture they have carefully crafted (the how).

If you want to

- reduce turnover, then pay attention to culture.
- raise the satisfaction level of your team, then pay attention to culture.
- get everyone rowing in the same direction, then pay attention to culture.
- differentiate yourself from others, then pay attention to culture.
- build a greater sense of team, then pay attention to culture.
- attract the right people to the team, then pay attention to culture.
- minimize sideways energy and dysfunction, then pay attention to culture.
- build a healthy and high-performing team, then pay attention to culture.

TEAM DISCUSSION QUESTIONS

1. What company or ministry do you think has a great culture? What are some of the defining qualities of their culture?
2. What are some of the defining qualities of your organization's culture? What words would you use to describe the culture of your team?
3. What is one quality you would like to see get stronger in your organization's culture?
4. How can clear and healthy culture minimize dysfunction?

31

Doing vs. Developing

Effective leaders work not only "in" the ministry but also "on" the ministry. Working in the ministry means you are the one executing the tasks and doing the actual work. Working on the ministry means stepping back from the tasks to work on developing the ministry. That requires time for forward thinking, strategic planning, and people development. Every single day in ministry you are faced with the tension of "doing" or "developing." I suspect that most of us default to doing instead of developing.

Doing vs. Developing

A few years ago, I read a blog post by Stephen Blandino on this topic of doing vs. developing.[1]

It made me start thinking about the contrast between the two. Below I have added to his list:

- Doing gets the job done; developing gets the job done through others.
- Doing is transactional; developing is transformational.
- Doing only measures results; developing also measures reproduction.
- Doing is about today; developing is about tomorrow.

- Doing looks at what you're accomplishing; developing looks at whom you're cultivating.
- Doing focuses on performance; developing focuses on people.
- Doing is about "what"; developing is about "who."
- Doing is fast; developing is slow.
- Doing is short-term thinking; developing is long-term thinking.

One of the most powerful ways of multiplying the capacity and impact of your ministry is to focus on people development. A developmental culture is a healthy culture. I am confident we would all agree that developing people is important, but it rarely seems to find its way into our calendar. Developing never feels urgent, so it is easy for it to become just an unrealized good intention.

I think another significant issue is that many of us have never really had a person invest in our own development. We may have been to school and received some kind of training, but that is different from someone spending one-on-one time to grow and develop us as leaders.

In recent years, I have come to the fundamental conviction that the multiplication of our ministry is dependent on our learning the skill of developing people. But most of us have grown up in ministry learning how to do instead of develop. We are better players than coaches. We like to be out on the field. We like to call the plays and direct the team. But coaches are all about developing people and getting the very best out of them. While players make plays, coaches make players.

If we want to have healthy teams, we have to learn the skills of a coach. A friend of mine taught me this valuable principle: "More time spent with fewer people equals greater impact." That certainly was Jesus's strategy. He found a handful of followers, and for three years He poured Himself into them and then left the future of the kingdom in their hands. The people you lead are your handful. If you went back and reviewed several years of my calendar, you would think I believed less time with more people equals greater impact. Not Jesus. He reserved the biggest blocks of time for pouring into His handful.

A number of years ago, I came to a crossroads in my ministry. After about fifteen years of being a pastor, I began to have a growing dissatisfaction with how we were doing church and how I was leading my team. Outwardly, everything looked great. The church was growing and morale was great. We had the reputation of being "the" church in town, and we had a great staff team. We had also come through a successful capital campaign. But I had this nagging sense that we weren't doing a very good job discipling and developing our people, including our staff members.

I also remember being captivated by a passage in 1 Thessalonians 2. In verse 7, Paul writes, "We were like a mother feeding and caring for her own children" (NLT). In verse 8, he says, "We shared with you not only God's Good News but our own lives, too" (NLT). Then in verses 11 and 12, we read, "And you know that we treated each of you as a father treats his own children. We pleaded with you, encouraged you, and urged you to live your lives in a way that God would consider worthy" (NLT).

This passage drips with relationship. And as a result, I am convinced that the best analogy of development is the parent-child relationship. Think of the similarities between developing those under your leadership and raising children. No book or class can really prepare you. You never feel adequate. It is slow and messy. Each child (or member of your team) is unique and different, so their development must be customized. And relationship provides you insight into what they need to grow.

Just as with your kids, at times you will have to use situational leadership. In 1 Thessalonians 2, Paul writes that as a spiritual father, there will be times when you encourage, times when you plead, and times when you urge/challenge.

Think about somebody you are responsible to lead. Get someone's name and face in your mind. How do you know when to encourage? Or when to comfort? Or when to challenge or confront them? It comes through relationship. The most fertile soil for development is the messy and time-consuming soil of relationship.

Developmental Questions

Let me give you three questions that will help you in developing the people in your ministry.

1. Who are they?

This is about really getting to know the person. What is their story? How are they wired? What are their passions? You can impress from a distance, but you impact up close and personal. Take the time to get into the lives of the people you lead.

2. Where are they?

This is about assessing and figuring out where they are in their journey and where they need to develop and grow. How is their job going? Where are they winning? Where are they stuck? What tools do they need to succeed? Where are some of the challenges?

3. How can I help them?

This is about coming alongside them and helping them take their next steps in growth and development. This is about modeling and coaching, encouraging and challenging, and then celebrating when growth happens. This is also about removing roadblocks to their growth and success.

If you are like me, you find it easy to see all your own shortcomings and feel inadequate to develop others. I can hear some of you saying, "I don't even have my own act together, so who am I to help develop others?"

Just being authentically interested in people's growth and development is 90 percent of the battle. Cut yourself some slack. You don't have to be perfect to be a good coach and developer of people. And just like parenting, you get a lot of your skill through on-the-job training. Someone once said that wisdom is seeing fifteen minutes into the future. If you can just be fifteen minutes ahead of your team, you can help them grow and develop.

Best Practices

1. Call people up.

One of the top leadership lessons from the legendary basketball coach John Wooden is to make greatness available to everyone. "A leader's greatness is found in bringing out greatness in others. Personal greatness is measured—like success—against one's own potential, not that of someone else."[2]

Potential is like a seed. It could lay stagnant and dormant. Or, with the right mixture of soil, light, fertilizer, and water, it can experience exponential growth. The same is true with people. Part of your job is to see the potential within people and then provide the right environment for them to develop.

2. Be like a personal trainer (but without the gym shorts).

What is it that personal trainers do? First, they are in close proximity. Personal trainers don't shout instructions from across the gym. They are right there watching, observing, cheerleading, and coaching. Second, trainers don't do the workouts for people they are coaching. I've never seen a trainer say, "Why don't you step aside and let me do your reps for you today?" Not a chance. Trainers know that the only way for someone to get stronger is for them to do the work themselves. Third, they take a crawl, walk, run approach. Good trainers always assess where a person is in their development and customize the training program to fit that person's current ability. Trainers lay out plans that are doable but stretching. You want to do the same with the people you are trying to develop.

3. Ask great questions.

"The skill of the coach is the art of questioning."[3]

If you want to be a great developer of people, learn the skill of being a curious listener. I have a couple of friends who are great at asking questions and being authentically interested in whomever they are talking to. They inspired me to start reflecting on the power and benefits of asking good questions.

- Questions are disarming and much less threatening than declarations.
- Questions communicate value and interest. When you ask me a question, you are asking for my opinion and input. And that feels good.
- Questions invite discussion. Instead of a top-down monologue, questions create the opportunity for dialogue.

241

- Questions assist in diagnosis. It is important to get the perspective of the person you are coaching and developing. When you go to the doctor, they ask questions that help them diagnose what's going on inside of you. Questions give you the added insight so you best know how to coach.

- Questions facilitate learning. When you ask my opinion and invite me into the process, I will take greater ownership. Self-discovery is always the best teacher, and questions are invaluable in facilitating self-discovery.

4. Provide real-time coaching.

The best coaching happens as close to the experience as possible. You see this all the time in football games. When the quarterback runs off the field after an offensive series, the coach will huddle up and provide some "in the moment" coaching.

In an article on delivering results and developing people, Wendy Axelrod and Jeanine Coyle write, "It's about seizing small everyday moments. Using quick, spontaneous acts, from giving on-the-fly feedback to turning mistakes into instant learning, is an effective way to develop people. You simply need to be attentive in the moment, resisting the urge to rush ahead to the next thing. The moments you 'sacrifice' now are an investment in your people and will ultimately lead to greater efficiency and effectiveness."[4]

5. Utilize one word.

If people development is something fairly new to you, let me give you an idea for a great way to get started. You will want to give this some thought ahead of time. Then I suggest you sit down with each person you have responsibility to lead and develop. Have a discussion about their development. Talk about identifying one word that would be the focus of their development in the coming year. Invite their input. Where do they think they need to grow and develop? This is also a time to provide your insight as to areas where they could grow.

Once you have agreed on a word (and it doesn't have to be in that initial meeting), find a Scripture verse that speaks to that developmental word.

For example, let's say you and that person agree that the developmental word for this coming year is *communication*. They want to grow in their skill as a speaker. Then it is your job to provide opportunities and experiences that will help them develop that skill. It could be a book or two, podcasts, a speaker's training event, and possibly coaching from you. It is also your job to keep this on the radar in the coming months.

Finding one word to focus on can be a powerful and simple way to have a developmental focus for the people you watch over.

Next Steps

Who is a person you should start developing? Who is the person you have your eye on who could take your place or carry a big chunk of the ministry?

Let me challenge you to get started. You could do something as simple as having lunch together and hearing their story. But make the decision now to get intentional about developing someone and make it a priority in your schedule. Sometimes that will mean dedicating time to developmental conversations. And sometimes it will mean facilitating developmental experiences.

Remember, the people you develop today will determine where your ministry is able to go tomorrow.

TEAM DISCUSSION QUESTIONS

1. Who invested in your development? What specifically did they do to help develop you?
2. Who on your team or in your ministry does a good job of developing others? How do they go about developing others?
3. Which of the following coaching qualities do you need to work on?

   - Call people up
   - Be like a personal trainer

- Ask great questions
- Provide real-time coaching
- Utilize "one" word

4. Whom do you need to be investing in? What next steps can you take with them?

32

Shock and Awe

Back when I was a kid, about the time dinosaurs were roaming the earth, every week at our church we had Wednesday Night Prayer Meeting. Obviously, this was before church marketing people came up with creative one-word names for ministries like Thrive, Crave, Elevate, Wake, or Shift. To be honest, it was the least exciting and most dreaded of all our church ministries. Apparently, I wasn't the only person in my church who felt this way, as reflected by how few people actually showed up.

Our prayer meetings lasted an hour, but it felt like time came to a complete standstill from seven to eight on Wednesday nights. Ninety-eight percent of all prayer requests were either job or health related. We prayed for a lot of broken hips and sprained ankles.

I don't ever remember any real passion or fervor in our prayer meetings. And our prayers were anything but faith filled and bold. As I reflect back, I don't think any of us actually expected anything to happen as a result of our prayers, which came more from a place of duty than delight. The word I would use to describe those prayer times is *boring*.

No wonder my personal prayer life floundered. Even as a pastor, prayer has always been a struggle. But there is also a biblical story that has been a catalyst for change in my personal and team prayer life. It is a story told by Jesus in Luke 11. The chapter opens with perhaps the most general,

245

vague, nondescript verse in all the Bible. It simply says, "One day Jesus was praying in a certain place."

Wow—talk about generic.

- "One day"—This doesn't tell us which day.
- "Jesus was praying"—We aren't told if He was standing, sitting, or kneeling. We aren't told how long He prayed or if He prayed with His eyes open or shut. There is no record of the words He prayed.
- "In a certain place"—There is no mention of where He was praying. We don't know if He was in a house or outside in a garden or at the synagogue.

But there must have been something gripping about observing Jesus in prayer. Because when He was finished praying, the disciples said, "Lord, teach us to pray" (Luke 11:1). This is the only time ever recorded when the disciples asked Jesus to teach them something. Jesus then launched into the well-known Lord's Prayer. Although the version in Luke is a little shorter than the one in Matthew, they are basically the same. These verses are really about the "what" of prayer. The Lord's Prayer helps us know the kinds of things we ought to pray about.

But Jesus knows there is another fundamental issue in prayer. It's not just about the words and the "what"; it's also about our attitudes and hearts. It's not just about saying the right words or speaking prayers that are theologically correct. To help us understand how to approach prayer, Jesus told a story.

> Then Jesus said to them, "Suppose you have a friend, and you go to him at midnight and say, 'Friend, lend me three loaves of bread; a friend of mine on a journey has come to me, and I have no food to offer him.' And suppose the one inside answers, 'Don't bother me. The door is already locked, and my children and I are in bed. I can't get up and give you anything.'" (Luke 11:5–7)

The punch line of the story comes in verse 8: "I tell you, even though he will not get up and give you the bread because of friendship, yet because of your *shameless audacity* he will surely get up and give you as much as you need" (emphasis added). It wasn't friendship that got the neighbor out of bed and throwing loaves of bread out the front door. No, it was boldness and "shameless audacity" that won the day.

I have my own twenty-first-century version of this story. Many years ago, I was the pastor of a small church in North Texas. To say our church was rural is a huge understatement. You couldn't get to our church without driving on a dirt road. One night after church I was driving home and had both kids with me. Connie was following behind us in her car. I was talking with the kids and didn't really notice that Connie wasn't behind us anymore.

She had stopped on one of those dirt roads to pick up a stray dog. She had seen the dog along the side of the road for a couple of days and decided she would bring it home as a pet for the family. She stopped the car, opened the passenger door, and the dog jumped right in.

As soon as the dog jumped into the car, Connie had a bad feeling and thought to herself, *This was a mistake.* She tried to coax the dog out of the car, but as she did, he snarled and growled at her. The car was running and the dog was now lying on her purse.

She then remembered that some of our church members lived on that dirt road about a half mile from where she was and decided her only option was to go ask them for help. She started walking on that dark road at about 10:30 at night, and as she walked, she began to hear sounds in the night. She now started to jog, and with each step she became more panicked. By the time she got to the house she was in a full run and crying.

She ran across their front lawn and yelled out, "Cathy, help me. Help me." As Connie got to the front door, the porch light flipped on. And as the door opened, there to greet Connie was Cathy's husband. Dripping wet, he couldn't have weighed 140 pounds, and he was standing there in all his glory. He had a gun in his hand and was not wearing anything but his black bikini underwear. But he was nice enough to help Connie (after getting his pants on) get the stray dog out of her car.

I promise this story does have a spiritual point. Connie had a real and serious need. And she knew and trusted that these church friends would help. So, she knocked on their door with shameless audacity.

And that's the point of the story in Luke 11. God invites us to come to Him with shameless audacity.

That might sound a little presumptuous, and maybe you're thinking, *I thought we were supposed to approach God humbly.* There is a difference in coming to God boldly and coming to God arrogantly. Hebrews 4:16 tells us, "So let us come boldly to the throne of our gracious God. There we will receive his mercy, and we will find grace to help us when we need it most" (NLT).

That is very different from how we prayed in the church where I grew up. We always prayed sheepishly, "God, if it's your will and you have time and you don't mind, if you could potentially, maybe, possibly hear my prayer." This story that Jesus told invites us to come boldly and with shameless audacity. When you are desperate, you don't worry about good manners or protocol or policy. You don't care about your image or what people will think.

When Jesus finished the story, He gave us this famous passage on prayer: "So I say to you: Ask and it will be given to you; seek and you will find; knock and the door will be opened to you. For everyone who asks receives; the one who seeks finds; and to the one who knocks, the door will be opened" (Luke 11:9–10). Unlike the grumpy neighbor, when you ask, seek, and knock in prayer, you have a loving heavenly Father who delights to respond. You are not bothering, disturbing, or annoying Him.

Think about this for a moment. Our great and majestic and holy and all-powerful God graciously invites us to boldly bring our needs before Him. All three of the key words are imperatives. They could accurately be translated, "Ask and keep on asking. Seek and keep on seeking. Knock and keep on knocking." God is inviting you to pound on heaven's door.

Let me challenge you to put this into practice personally and with your team:

- Schedule an hour in your calendar every week for dedicated prayer. For me, this requires that I get out of my office. I am too easily distracted by all the stuff that needs to be done. Going to a separate room in the church or just walking and praying is very helpful for me.
- Dedicate time in your team meetings for prayer. Being a type A personality, I like meetings that start on time, follow an organized agenda,

have clear decisions and action steps, and end on time. Consequently, the idea of dedicating a half hour every week to prayer felt counter-intuitive. But doing so ended up being a rich and spiritually fruitful experience for our team.

- Develop a personal prayer team. Since the apostle Paul was not bash-ful about asking people to pray for him, I decided that I shouldn't be either. I recruited a handful of people who I knew were people of prayer and asked them to be on my personal prayer team. We tried to come together once a week during lunch, and the sole purpose was for this team to pray about the concerns and needs in my life. I know my life and ministry were better and more effective because of the faithfulness of these intercessors.

- Divide your team up into prayer partners for thirty days. Ask them to pray together a few days a week for the next month.

- Practice worship-based prayer. "Worship-based prayer seeks the face of God before the hand of God. God's face is the essence of who He is. God's hand is the blessing of what He does."[1] Daniel Henderson's book *Transforming Prayer* is a great resource to help your team have fresh and meaningful encounters in prayer.

- Read great books on prayer and study the prayers of Scripture. Con-sider doing this together as a team. This has been instrumental in fueling our team's passion for prayer. It has also been instructive to study the prayers of the Bible and to notice how different they are from the kinds of prayers we tend to pray.

- Pray with people, not just for people. Make it part of your team culture to regularly stop and pray "in the moment." So often we glibly tell people we will pray for them, but then life gets busy and we forget. Why not stop right in the middle of a meeting or in the middle of a conversation and take that need to God.

Start making prayer a greater priority. Start praying big, bold, bodacious prayers. Start praying with greater fervor and passion. Start praying with anticipation and faith.

I love this little prayer I came across the other day: "Lord, I crawled across the barrenness to you with my empty cup, uncertain of asking for any small drop of refreshment. If only I had known you better, I would have come running with a bucket."[2]

May you and your team learn the joyful discipline of running to God with a bucket.

TEAM DISCUSSION QUESTIONS

1. How would you describe the health and vibrancy of your prayer life?
2. What word would you use to explain the current place of prayer in your team?
3. What practical step could you and your team take to make prayer a greater priority?
4. What current burden or need can you bring before God with shameless audacity?

33

Growing Christians, Not Just Leaders

had a really interesting conversation this week with a pastor I know quite well. He has been recovering from a recent surgery, and that has given him some unhurried space to reflect, think, hear, *be*.

During his forced slow-down, this pastor told me he had been pondering a question. How would his life look different if he focused more on being a Christian and less on being a pastor? You might read that question and think to yourself, *Well, of course we should focus more on our identity as Christians than on our position as ministers.* One is about the foundation of our "being" and the other is about the function of our "doing." One is about our position in Christ, and the other is about our position in ministry. One is permanent; one is temporary.

But if you have been in ministry very long, you know how easy it is to get the two intertwined. When you feel called, and when you have great passion for ministry, the lines between person and position can get fuzzy. You move from simply being a Christian to being a professional Christian.

In 2 Timothy 3, when Paul is talking about the end times, he speaks of those who have a form of godliness but deny its power. That reality is not limited to those who are far from God. It can also be the reality of those who speak for God. When that becomes true, you move into image management. What you project on the outside isn't what you are experiencing on the inside, and that is a dangerous place for a leader in ministry. When you focus only on being a leader and not on being a Christian, you begin to neglect your own relationship with Christ. And before long you find yourself leading on empty, and that's a dead-end street. No one else may know what is going on inside you (at least for a while), but you begin to feel the disconnect. There is a hollowness to how you are doing life and ministry.

I believe one of the things that will help mitigate that unhealthy trajectory is to bring spiritual formation into the life of your team. In other words, make it a priority to help yourself and those on your team be better Christians, not just better leaders and pastors.

I once heard James Houston ask an insightful question about this issue. He asked, "Do you want to be successful or righteous?" The truth is, for much of my ministry, my deepest desire was to be successful. Looking back, I can see it clearly now—my ambition was in the driver's seat and my formation took a back seat. There's nothing wrong with ambition when it is motivated by God's glory, but it should flow out of a healthy, humble, and connected soul. Otherwise, your ambition will be overtaken by your ego.

We can never stop paying attention to our own sanctification. Someone once posed the question, "How long does it take to become a Christian?" And the answer is "a moment and a lifetime." At the moment of conversion, you are instantly born again, and the Bible says you are made a new creation. However, it is also true that you will spend the rest of your life on a journey toward Christlikeness. As Martin Luther is credited as having said, "A Christian is never in a state of completion but always in the process of becoming."

In the healthiest teams, the focus is on being and becoming as much as it is on doing. As a leader you must have the spiritual formation of the team you lead on your radar. One common mistake I see is that leaders assume those on their team are growing and thriving spiritually. I can tell you from working with hundreds of teams, that assumption just isn't true.

The result is that little or no time is dedicated to the spiritual development of the team members.

I think leaders must ask themselves, "Do I really believe that what God anoints and blesses is purity, holiness, humility, prayer, dependence, and

Christlikeness?" If the real spiritual power doesn't lie in our intellect or strategic gifts or talent or speaking ability but in abiding in Christ, doesn't it make sense that we would spend time as a team learning how to abide? Our walk with Christ should inform our work for Christ.

I think the apostle Paul would agree. In 1 Timothy 4:7–8, he writes, "Have nothing to do with godless myths and old wives' tales; rather, train yourself to be godly. For physical training is of some value, but godliness has value for all things, holding promise for both the present life and the life to come." He didn't say, "Train yourself to be strategic or train yourself to cast vision." Your first priority is to train yourself in godliness.

I think John Ortberg must have been thinking about these verses when he wrote, "Spiritual transformation is not a matter of trying harder, but training wisely."[1]

What is the spiritual training program for you and your team?

Too often spiritual disciplines are presented as a purely individual experience. But there is power in spiritual practices being experienced in community. Paul writes, "Let the message of Christ dwell among you richly as you teach and admonish one another with all wisdom through psalms, hymns, and songs from the Spirit, singing to God with gratitude in your hearts" (Col. 3:16). When Paul challenges the Colossian believers to "let the message of Christ dwell among you," the "you" in verse 16 is you plural (y'all for you southern folks). Then he goes on to list spiritual practices they can experience in community.

Even in Jesus's darkest hour, He did not go to Gethsemane alone. He took Peter, James, and John. And even though He went off in solitude to pray, He asked the three men to stay and pray. We are not sure exactly why, but Jesus came back to where He had left the disciples. In fact, He returned to His friends three different times. Jesus certainly had an individual experience as He prayed that this cup would be taken from Him, but He also wanted to experience something that night in community with His disciples.

In Mark 6, Jesus had sent out the twelve disciples to preach the gospel, cast out demons, and heal the sick. After that busy ministry assignment, the Bible says the disciples came back together and reported to Jesus all that had been done. "And He said to them, 'Come away by yourselves to

253

a secluded place and rest a while.' (For there were many people coming and going, and they did not even have time to eat.)" (Mark 6:31 NASB).

I like the phrase "come away." The ministry matters. The work matters. But there is a time to "come away" for rest and replenishment. It is the rhythm of engagement and disengagement. You need times when the team can "come away" from the demands and drains of ministry to be spiritually refilled.

I remember hearing Gary Haugen from International Justice Mission (IJM) talk about this and how his organization has made "coming away" a priority. He said the laws of the spiritual world are organized in such a way that God shows up most powerfully when we need Him most desperately. He said we are not only trying to do a hard thing in bringing the kingdom to our world, but we are also doing it as flawed and needy people, which puts us in a place of desperate need for God.

Because Gary absolutely believes that to be true, IJM has created space for team members to seek and experience God. And they do it while on the clock. I'm not sure what their practice is now, but at that time the entire team started their day at 8:30 a.m. with a half hour of stillness. Before the doors swung open, the emails started flying, and the phones started ringing, everyone spent the first half hour of the morning in prayer and reflection. That time was set aside to be with God and prepare spiritually for what was coming that day.

Let me give you a few ideas that might stimulate your thinking about how to raise your team's spiritual temperature.

- *Open the Word*. Read a passage together and talk about it. Have someone begin your meeting with a devotion. Share a verse or passage that God used to speak to you.
- *Lectio Divina (sacred reading)*. Select a passage of Scripture and read it through out loud a couple of times. This is about lingering over a passage. Ask people to share their observations and what stands out to them from the passage. And then take a few moments to talk about any personal application from the passage. This is an excellent way to experience the power of Scripture in community.

- *Daily Office.* The Daily Office is an opportunity to have a brief connection with God during your day. My friend Pete Scazzero has an impressive collection of these in his book *Emotionally Healthy Spirituality Day by Day.*[2] The Daily Office begins with a couple of minutes of silence. That is followed by a Scripture reading and very short devotional. Then there is a question to consider and a written prayer. The Daily Office concludes with another couple of minutes of silence. It takes about ten minutes to complete the Daily Office, but it is a powerful way to connect with God during your day.

- *Dedicated times of prayer.* Rather than the obligatory opening or closing prayer, why not consider having a half hour of prayer? Or scheduling an hour-long prayer meeting to intercede for the needs of the ministry?

- *Worship songs.* Recently I was teaching a group of pastors at a retreat. At the end of the session, one of the men in the group said, "There is a worship song I've been listening to that fits perfectly with the teaching we just heard." He cued up the song and we all sat there and had a powerful spiritual moment as the song ministered to us.

- *Days of personal retreat.* Two churches and ministries I know give people a day or two a year for personal retreat. It is not a day off, but it is a day to spend with Jesus. I like the thought of having a template people can use to guide their day. I also like providing different readings or ideas people can employ to facilitate a meaningful personal retreat.

- *Fasting.* Fasting can be a rich and powerful experience when you do it as a ministry or team. Fasting specifically for a particular spiritual need or opportunity can be a wonderful way to galvanize your team.

- *Silence.* Consider starting a staff meeting with a couple of minutes of silence. If you've never done this before, two minutes can seem like twenty. We're so used to having constant noise that silence can feel awkward and unsettling. But silence allows us to slow ourselves down, to become quiet before the Lord, and to better discern His still, small voice.

- *Journaling.* Personally, I do not journal very consistently. I know it is a valuable practice, but I have always struggled to maintain any regularity. However, I've had some meaningful experiences when I've

255

done journaling exercises as part of a group experience. Sometimes I will give a staff team a set of questions. Then I have them scatter and find a place where they can be alone for thirty minutes. I then tell them to pray and ask God which question He wants them to journal about. At the end of the half hour, everyone comes back together and people share how God showed up during their journaling time. I am always amazed at what people reveal.

- *Soul care book.* I know many teams that regularly go through some kind of leadership book together. I want to give you a challenge. For every leadership book you go through, work through a book that focuses on feeding your soul.
- *Technology-free meetings or days.* I know this sounds crazy for a bunch of technology addicts. But what if you had an occasional technology-free day (no cell phones, text messages, or social media) at work and focused on being present with one another and with God?

Let me close by taking you back to my friend's question. How would your life and ministry look different if you focused more on being a Christian and less on being a ministry leader? What if you focused as much on knowing God as serving Him? What if you spent time on what you are becoming and not just what you are doing? What if your team spent as much energy on being "righteous" as you do on being "successful"?

TEAM DISCUSSION QUESTIONS

1. How would your days and weeks look different if you focused more on just being a Christian instead of being a leader?

2. When you hear the phrase "train yourself for godliness" (1 Tim. 4:7 ESV) what comes to mind?

3. What would it take for your team to be spiritually vibrant?

4. Of the practical ideas mentioned in this chapter, which one could your team immediately start putting into practice?

34

Becoming a CCO

You may have never heard of a little country called Bhutan. But in the 1970s, the king of Bhutan rejected the conventional paradigm of measuring cultural progress by the GDP. The GDP is the gross domestic product and is one of the primary indicators used to gauge the health of a country's economy. It represents the total dollar value of all goods and services produced over a specific time period.

Bhutan opted for a different kind of culture, and so it established the GNH, which stands for the Gross National Happiness index. The index has thirty-three indicators in nine different domains that measure contentment and happiness among the people of Bhutan.

As you can imagine, Bhutan's culture is radically different from America's consumer culture. Rather than being swept along by the global economic engine, Bhutan chose a different set of values to define its culture. The country's leaders were very intentional and followed the values of their core beliefs rather than letting someone else dictate what their values should be. I also love that Bhutan established an instrument to help measure what the people truly valued. The result is that in 2015, only 8.8 percent of Bhutanese people described themselves as unhappy. The leaders of Bhutan have carefully crafted a culture that reflects the values of their beliefs.

Dharmesh Shah, the cofounder of the company Hubspot, writes, "In our early years, we didn't talk about culture much. We hadn't documented it at all. We just built a business that we wanted to work in. And, that was great. But the real return on culture happened when we started getting more deliberate about it. By writing it down. By debating it. By taking it apart, polishing the pieces and putting it back together. Iterating. Again. And again."[1]

Healthy Culture vs. Toxic Culture

I know you can't lump all cultures together and create a stereotype. But in my forty years of being around ministry and ministry leaders, I do think some general characteristics typify healthy cultures and toxic cultures.

Healthy Culture	Toxic Culture
Life-giving	Life-draining
Spoken cultural values	Unspoken cultural values
Respect for leaders	Resentment for leaders
Transparency	Image management
Genuine	Disingenuous
High trust	Low trust
Optimism	Cynicism
Energy directed toward vision	Energy directed toward dysfunction
Clarity	Confusion
Humility	Hubris
Lower turnover	Higher turnover
Own your mistakes	Blame and deflect
Faith-filled	Fear-filled
Values people	Uses people
Candid feedback	Guarded feedback
Driven by purpose	Driven by personality
Honest communication	"Spin" communication
Abundance mentality	Scarcity mentality

The truth is, no organization always lives in the healthy culture column. And I've never been around a ministry that was 100 percent toxic. The two columns represent the absolutes, and we don't live in the absolute. We usually live somewhere in between. But we want to keep moving toward the markers and behaviors of a healthy culture.

By the way, you may already be concluding that you work in a toxic culture. Maybe you are already beginning to mentally point the finger of blame at someone else. I just want to remind you that while you may not be in control of the entire organization, you do have influence over the part of the organization where you serve. Instead of looking outward, I encourage you to look inward. "Be the change" you want in your church or ministry culture.

Crafting a Healthy Culture

Naming and articulating the desired culture is only the start. It has to move from words to walk. It has to move from articulation to action.

Implementing your desired culture begins with ownership and intentionality. Consider yourself the CCO—the chief culture officer of whatever piece of the ministry you are responsible for. That means you must understand, champion, advocate for, protect, and model the key values of the culture you desire. In the most high-performing cultures, everyone owns and embodies the key distinctives.

As the person in charge of your department, it might help to see yourself as not only the CCO but also as the master gardener. You must learn how to have a "green thumb" for growing a healthy and high-performing culture. That means you are constantly seeding, nurturing, weeding, watering, inspecting, and looking for disease.

There is a huge difference between nurturing culture and mandating or whiteboarding it. In other words, handing down an edict or simply having a culture brainstorming session isn't helpful when it comes to creating a winsome culture. Someone in senior leadership can hand down a culture mandate, but the truth is, healthy cultures are built from the inside out. People have to believe it, see it, feel it, and be inspired by it before they will own it. You don't mandate your people into being "raving fans." External compliance will never truly create a healthy culture. It is an inside job. It has to incubate inside the hearts of the team members and ultimately hatch into new behaviors and habits. Healthy culture is better caught than taught.

Creating culture is not just about handing out a list of desired behaviors. People need to be inspired. They need to understand the "why" behind the behaviors. They need to hear compelling stories and see the potential of what "could be." And they need to witness what it looks like in the everyday life of your ministry.

If you think your ministry culture could use a makeover, let me give you a piece of advice that I have had to learn the hard way. Don't form a huddle with a few key leaders and come up with the new and improved culture plan. Gather input. Be inclusive and collaborative. And especially don't have a big fanfare moment as you announce the rollout of the new culture.

In a case study about culture change in a thirty-three-year-old pharmaceutical company called Dr. Reddy's, the company created a new purpose statement of just four words: "Good health can't wait." "But instead of plastering this new slogan on motivational posters and repeating it in all-hands meetings, the leadership team began by quietly using it to start guiding their own decisions. The goal was to *demonstrate* this idea in action, not talk about it."[2]

It's not enough to simply create a list of cultural values and behaviors you want. As a leader, you must *be* the change you want in the ministry. Your organizational and personal behaviors as a leader either underscore or undermine the culture you desire. Your actions either elevate or erode what you are trying to build. For example, if you want a culture of innovation, you can't give people the smackdown when they try something new and then fail.

Developing a Spiritually Rich Culture

In the previous chapter, I mentioned that leaders should focus on creating a healthy and life-giving culture for those on their team. In ministry organizations, part of culture development should also include spiritual transformation.

Often those in senior leadership assume their staff members are growing spiritually outside of their role in the ministry. In my experience working with ministry teams, I can tell you that is not a safe assumption. The primary differentiator between a healthy secular culture and a healthy ministry culture is the focus on spiritual transformation. Many of the values companies articulate, such as integrity, collaboration, and self-improvement, could and should be embraced by all organizations. But one area of focus that makes churches and ministry organizations distinctively Christian is that we intentionally concentrate on the spiritual development of our staff members, both as individuals and as a team.

I hope you are committed to engaging the spiritual lives of those in your ministry organization. Again, this comes down to behaviors. In a spiritually healthy culture, we help our people engage in spiritual practices that result in loving communion with God. If something is truly a value, it has to show up in what we talk about, how we spend our time, and what we do together.

Do It

Hopefully as you read this chapter, you will identify some things you can do to build a robust ministry culture. Here is a simple (not easy) eight-step process for moving toward a healthy culture.

Prioritize It

You personally, and your organization, have limited bandwidth. When it comes to culture, you will have to make a value judgment as to its importance and priority. It will never feel urgent, but I believe it is crucially important. As Tony Hsieh says, "As it turns out, it doesn't actually matter what your company's core values are. What matters is that you have them and that you commit to them. What's important is the alignment that you get from them when they become the default way of thinking for the entire organization."[3]

Articulate It

Sit down with the people in your ministry to have discussions about the kind of culture you desire. These conversations can and should take some time. Be sure to get input from people all across your ministry. Narrow your list down to the handful of key culture behaviors/values that you want to be the distinctives of your ministry. Once you have the key values identified, wordsmith them to make them as clear and concise as possible.

Inspire It

Cast vision for what a healthy culture would mean and the impact it could have. Talk about the "why." Tell stories, give examples, and paint a picture of a compelling and life-giving culture.

Model It

A great team culture starts with you. It can't be "them" or "those people in senior leadership." It has to start with you personally. Regularly ask yourself, "Do my decisions, words, attitudes, and actions reflect our desired culture?" As basketball icon Michael Jordan is purported to have said, "Some people want it to happen, some wish it would happen, others make it happen."

Integrate It

Think holistically. Ask yourself in regard to your ministry: How should these culture behaviors/values impact our hiring process? How should they impact our meetings? How should they impact my development of volunteers? How should they impact my daily interaction with other team members? Ultimately, you want to have these values infiltrate and infect every facet of your ministry.

Drip It

Building culture requires a long-term view. Culture changes not because of a quick splash but rather because of a slow drip. Changing culture requires patience and tenacity. How can you drip it into conversations? How can you drip it into volunteer training? Team meetings? Project execution? Email? Systems and processes?

Celebrate It

Catch people doing something right. Highlight and celebrate behavior that reflects the culture you want. When people "get it," write them a personal note or give them a public pat on the back.

Guard It

People's memory is very strong. All of us have the tendency to go back to our default ways of thinking and behaving. Vigilance is a virtue—especially when you are trying to build a new culture. The culture of any organization is shaped by the worst behavior the leader is willing to tolerate. At times you will have to address behaviors that are contrary to the culture you are trying to build. How you handle those moments is crucial. You don't want people to feel like you are "calling them out" on their old behavior but rather that you are "calling them up" to a new culture.

When it comes to building a new culture, I love the sentiment captured by an unknown author:

> If you want to build a ship,
> don't drum up the people
> to gather wood, divide the
> work, and give orders.
>
> Instead, teach them to yearn
> for the vast and endless sea.

An old Chinese proverb says, "The best day to plant an oak was twenty years ago. The second best day is today."

So, get started today building a life-giving team culture.

TEAM DISCUSSION QUESTIONS

1. What are some practical ways you can become a champion for a healthy culture?
2. From the healthy culture list earlier in this chapter, what is one quality you believe is true of your organization's culture? What is one characteristic from the toxic culture list that you need to be aware of?
3. What are some mechanisms within your organization that you can use to "drip in" healthy culture (for example, staff meetings)?
4. What does it look like to guard a healthy culture? Why is this so important?

35

Culture Tensions

Ministry first and foremost is a spiritual enterprise. We are not trying to build a successful business or increase profits or capture market share, we are trying to grow a beautiful bride.

> For husbands, this means love your wives, just as Christ loved the church. He gave up his life for her to make her holy and clean, washed by the cleansing of God's word. He did this to present her to himself as a glorious church without a spot or wrinkle or any other blemish. Instead, she will be holy and without fault. (Eph. 5:25–27 NLT)

Marriage is a visible demonstration of the relationship between Christ and His bride—the church. Notice the words that are used to characterize this beautiful bride:

- Love
- Holy
- Clean
- Washed
- Without spot
- Without wrinkle
- Without blemish
- Without fault

They are not quantity words; they are quality words. They are not business words; they are bride words.

In light of that truth, I have a growing concern as I observe ministries. My concern is that we are being conditioned to lead as the world does. We shouldn't just baptize best business practices and sprinkle in some God language. I am a fan of learning from anyone we can (including business leaders), but we must never forget we are most importantly a spiritual organization. And because that's true, we do things differently.

We should lead from a different place—a place of spiritual depth and a sense of God's power and presence that transcends best business practices. We aren't trying to sell a product or earn a profit for the company. We are about making disciples and creating a beautiful bride.

We should honestly evaluate whether our leadership lines up with how Jesus modeled it. Are kingdom values reflected in how we do our work and lead our teams? Are we doing things the "Jesus" way?

We must hold four tensions to create a beautiful-bride culture.

Andy Stanley talks about the fact that in life and in ministry, some things aren't problems to be solved; they are tensions to be managed.[1] And I believe those in healthy cultures have learned to manage these four tensions.

Work Hard vs. Unplug Hard

In my ministry, Replenish, I often teach about the practice of Sabbath. In Exodus 20:9, when God was giving the command to observe the Sabbath, He said, "Six days you shall labor and do all your work." It is God's expectation that we are productive. In other words, on the days you are supposed to work, get after it. Be diligent. Bring your A game. Go all in. Don't fritter away the day on social media and hallway conversations. As ministry leaders we should have a strong work ethic.

The healthiest churches have a cultural value of hard work and hold people accountable for being productive—and at the very same time they value Sabbath and rest and time for family.

To be healthy, you need a life outside of ministry. Jesus is your life, but ministry is not your entire life. Jesus made you a human before he made you a ministry leader. And you have all the same needs and limitations as any other human.

265

As I have already talked about, there is a God-ordained rhythm that allows us to live and lead from a healthy soul. That rhythm is work, then rest. Produce, then replenish. Go hard, then stop. Empty your bucket, then fill your bucket.

That means you need to have interests and hobbies outside of ministry. When I was serving as an executive pastor at Saddleback, I took my workaholism to a whole new level. All I did was ministry and family. I did little to really invest in my marriage, and I did nothing to care for myself as a person. My kids often got the leftover scraps of a depleted dad. And I lost interest in all recreation and hobbies. I remember when someone would call me and invite me to play golf, my mental response was, "Do you know how much work I can get done in the four hours it would take to play a round of golf?" I had an unhealthy mind-set, and it took its toll on me.

I remember hearing Mark Miller, a vice president with Chick-fil-A, speak to a group of church leaders at a church staff meeting in West Palm Beach, Florida. In his talk he mentioned that when we are born, God gives us a palette of paints with which to paint a beautiful life. Then he pointedly said, "The problem I have observed with people in ministry is that they only paint with one color—the ministry color."

Part of what makes this a challenge is that you love what you do, and you have a sense of divine calling. But you will be a better ministry leader if you learn to have a healthy rhythm of working hard and unplugging hard.

Achieve vs. Abide (External vs. Internal)

According to John 15, the secret to spiritual power is "abiding." It is being in a loving and life-giving relationship with Jesus. But if you've been in ministry longer than a month, you know it is possible to show up and competently do your ministry without abiding in Christ.

It is easy to let your work *for* God replace your being *with* God. To me, it is like a husband who works excessively to make a great living so he and his wife can live in a big house in a nice neighborhood and drive a luxury SUV and have a robust 401(k). He justifies his compulsive pace because he has convinced himself he is doing it for his family. Yet he spends little time with his wife and relationally they have drifted apart.

I have experienced seasons when I have worked really hard to build the ministry but have done so to the neglect of relationship with the very One I am building the ministry for. As I look back, I can see clearly that at times runaway ambition was the driving motive in my life. Honestly, I cared about succeeding and being seen as a success more than I did about nurturing my relationship with Jesus. Jesus said, "I am the vine, you are the branches; he who abides in Me and I in him, he bears much fruit, for apart from Me you can do nothing" (John 15:5 NASB).

Spiritual life always flows from the inside to the outside, from the invisible to the visible, from the root to the fruit. Have you ever noticed that there is always a lag time between the branches not getting nourishment and the fruit drying up? That lag time is dangerous, because while the spiritual life has stopped flowing, we have the appearance of fruit. We eventually become like trees that are rotting from the inside. You can't tell that anything is wrong on the outside. But those trees are easily toppled by a storm.

Spirit vs. Systems

It seems as though ministries have a hard time finding the middle ground on this one. Most ministries lean heavily in one direction or the other. I think we all understand the value of systems. The human body is a complex web of systems: nerves, muscles, bones, and so on. Without those systems, the body couldn't function. They each have a certain amount of structure and control built into them. But one beautiful thing about the systems of the human body is that they were designed to allow mobility and flexibility. They actually facilitate movement.

But in some ministry environments, the systems and processes have become arthritic. They are now rigid and inflexible, and movement is painful. You know things have gotten unhealthy when the systems stop serving the team and start being served by the team.

I work with some multisite churches, and the other day I met with a campus pastor. His perception was that their systems had become rigid and inflexible, which led to increased frustration and decreased freedom. I don't know if his assessment was completely accurate, but I know in a system-heavy culture, you have to be careful not to remove all flexibility. Personally, I am wired to focus on systems. I love order and clarity.

In my years at Saddleback, I worked with Rick Warren, who has an incredible intuitive leadership gift. In his book *The Purpose-Driven Church*, Rick writes about the art of catching waves. When the right wave comes, you have to jump on it and ride it, not call a "catch the wave" planning meeting. People who are Spirit people "feel" a wave coming. They have an intuitive ability to discern and move when the Spirit prompts.[2] One of Rick's highest values was being able to turn on a dime. When he discerned a Holy Spirit moment for our church, he wanted to be able to jump on the wave and ride it *now*! This process was always messy but often yielded great kingdom fruit.

During my years at Saddleback, the "process" staff members were regularly frustrated and often didn't last very long. Those of us on staff would kiddingly say, "If you don't like organized religion, you are going to love our church." Because at times things could feel very unorganized. You had to have a high tolerance for ambiguity to thrive in that culture. It wasn't the right environment for those who needed to always have a plan and to stick to the plan.

Arthritic systems lead to lack of freedom and creativity. People feel handcuffed and stymied. In ministries that are only about catching the next wave, their lack of systems often leads to chaos and squandered fruit. People feel exhausted and stressed.

Think about an apple orchard. When God brings the fruit, the farmer needs a plan and a system for harvesting it. Otherwise, the fruit will just rot out in the field. When God sends a spiritual harvest, you need a system to capture and preserve the harvest. Both systems and spirit are absolutely necessary for a healthy team. It isn't that one group is spiritual and the other unspiritual. And as a leader, you want to learn to appreciate the strengths of both types of people.

Fruitfulness vs. Faithfulness

When I first started in ministry, the spotlight was clearly on the faithfulness side of the equation as opposed to the fruitfulness side. Over and over as a young pastor, I was challenged to be faithful to my call and leave the results to God. Years ago, Eugene Peterson wrote a book called *A Long Obedience in the Same Direction*. Not exactly a sexy title, but it does capture the spirit of the word *faithfulness*.

A generation ago, when pastors went to conferences or denominational conventions, the sermons were about prayer, holiness, evangelism, humility, revival, the cross, and staying true to your call. And then leadership and church growth hit the Christian culture like a tsunami. It wasn't long before every conference was about leadership, vision, and strategies for growth. The megachurch arrived on the scene. Pastors started consuming business leadership books like breath mints.

If a generation ago the focus was completely on faithfulness, today the pendulum has swung completely the other way. We have become obsessed with fruitfulness and leadership and vision. Many young leaders in ministries have grown up drinking the jet fuel of bigger and more. And I know from firsthand experience, it is intoxicating. However, I believe the healthiest teams live with the tension of seeking to be fruitful but also putting a high premium on faithfulness.

We like to quote passages such as Acts 17, which speaks of the early church turning the world upside down. We love to talk about great leaders who changed their generation. Our vision juices get flowing when we read in Hebrews 11 about great men and women who conquered kingdoms, shut the mouths of lions, quenched the fury of the flames, became powerful in battle, routed foreign armies, and even raised the dead to life. That's great fodder for conference sessions.

But I'm so glad the chapter doesn't end there. Otherwise, we would be tempted to think faith is always about victory, growth, success, and miracles. We would shine the spotlight on the exponential potential of faith and leave faithfulness in the dark. But thank God the middle of verse 35 takes a ninety-degree turn: "Women received back their dead, raised to life again. There were others who were tortured, refusing to be released so that they might gain an even better resurrection." The transition is subtle, but the generic word *others* begins to turn the spotlight from visionary faith to humble faithfulness.

As if to highlight their humility, the writer of Hebrews doesn't name these "others." This side of heaven they will remain anonymous. They

269

might be unknown in the Bible, but they are well-known in heaven. They might be anonymous, but their faith was courageous. So great was their faith that "the world was not worthy of them" (v. 38). Their faith and faithfulness didn't bring fame; it brought danger. And following Jesus did not bring notoriety; it brought obscurity.

Interestingly, "These were all commended for their faith, yet none of them received what had been promised" (v. 39). Not one of them received what had been promised. *Not yet.* Not in this world. Not all God's promises are fulfilled in this life. In a culture that is all about growth and impact and expansion and success, one of the most difficult places to live is a place called "not yet."

Here is what I know for sure. You don't ultimately control fruitfulness. A lot of factors impact the external results of your ministry. Location, history, infighting, funding, programs, staffing, community fit, receptivity in the community, God's favor—and the list goes on and on. But you have 100 percent absolute control over your personal faithfulness.

And remember, Jesus never said, "Well done, good and fruitful servant." He said, "Well done, good and *faithful* servant" (Matt. 25:23).

TEAM DISCUSSION QUESTIONS

1. How well do you balance working hard and unplugging hard? What would help you do this better?

2. Mark Miller said that when you were born, God gave you a palette of colors to paint a beautiful life. What is something you enjoy doing outside of ministry that helps you paint a beautiful life?

3. Honestly, how are you doing at pursuing your relationship with Jesus?

4. Complete the following statement: For me, faithfulness in my role means . . .

36

It's All about Behavior

What's commonly referred to as The Netflix Culture Manifesto is a wildly popular document on the internet with over eleven million views. At the beginning of their robust culture document, Netflix unashamedly declares the kind of organizational culture they want to have. But their declaration goes beyond hopes and wishes and inspiring platitudes. It spotlights specific behaviors that reinforce the desired culture. Here is a sample:

> Like all great companies, we strive to hire the best and we value integrity, excellence, respect, and collaboration.
> What is special about Netflix, though, is how much we:
>
> - Encourage independent decision-making by employees
> - Share information openly, broadly, and deliberately
> - Are extraordinarily candid with each other
> - Keep only our highly effective people
> - Avoid rules
>
> Our core philosophy is people over process.[1]

One specific value on which the Netflix culture is built is the pillar of communication. But the company doesn't leave it to the employees' imaginations to define what communication means at Netflix. Specific behaviors define what the value looks like day to day:

Communication

- You are concise and articulate in speech and writing
- You listen well and seek to understand before reacting
- You maintain calm poise in stressful situations to draw out the clearest thinking
- You adapt your communication style to work well with people from around the world who may not share your native language
- You provide candid, timely feedback to colleagues[2]

I love the specificity of those statements. They set clear behavioral expectations. So many of the value words we talk about are broad, vague, and open to a lot of different interpretations. The best leadership behaviors/values statements are clear, concise, and compelling. It is helpful to define in more granular terms what those value words look like in the everyday life of the organization.

What creates confusion and dysfunction in ministries and organizations is unclear expectations—a kind of organizational fog. And here's what I know to be true of fog: it slows you down and creates stress, because you can't really see where you're going. Instead of enjoying the ride, you are just trying to stay out of the ditch. That would describe how many people feel when trying to successfully navigate a ministry organization. While a good number of churches and ministries have a mission statement and some organizational values, they usually stop short of naming the leadership behaviors and values they expect from the staff.

In his book *Church Unique*, Will Mancini observes, "Collaboration is lost to sideways energy every day in the local church. Why? The three reasons I see most are mistrust, personal ego, and lack of strategic clarity. . . . Leaders rarely clarify what working together really looks like."[3]

Name It, Claim It

When I say "name it, claim it," I am not talking about the prosperity gospel. I am talking about naming and declaring specifically the kind of leadership behaviors and values you expect from those who lead in your organization. You are seeking to define your ministry's unique leadership DNA. Doing so allows the fog to lift.

It also helps you define staff training topics and how to vet potential hires.

If you don't currently have a clear set of leadership values and behaviors, I would suggest making this a collaborative and unhurried exercise. In a conversation I had with Rick Holliday from North Point Community Church in the Atlanta area, he talked about his church's process of articulating their Staff Covenant (their version of leadership behaviors). He said, "We took our time. We spent six months getting input, assessing, articulating, rewriting and creating questions about our leadership behaviors."

I would also suggest making this a collaborative exercise across the entire ministry organization. If the team is going to "stack hands" and really live by these, they need to have meaningful input. Also, when everyone participates, it allows people to articulate the values and expectations that are important to them in doing team. The process obviously needs to be guided by senior leadership, but the thoughtful input of people across the organization can be valuable.

This is not a tactical discussion. You aren't trying to solve a problem. You are trying to discern and discover the leadership values and behaviors that already exist to some degree but most likely have never been articulated and written down. Most often these leadership values are a reflection of senior leadership. You might begin by asking, "What really matters to our leaders? What are their personal leadership behaviors and values?"

Sometimes a good way to discover a value is to ask your team members, "What makes you pound your fist on the table? What makes you angry?" Sometimes people react strongly in a situation because a value has been violated.

It is also helpful to brainstorm a leadership behavior or two that isn't very strong in your culture right now but that you authentically value and want to be part of what defines your culture. I often refer to those as aspirational values/behaviors. By declaring a specific behavior a value, you

273

help keep that value on the radar and the team will be more accountable for living it out. You don't want more than a couple of these, but having one or two you want to work on is great.

This isn't one of those exercises that, when you are done, you just file away to never look at again. It should be a living document that you review regularly, use in one-on-one conversations, share in team meetings, articulate when onboarding a new team member, and occasionally teach during staff meetings. This is not a marketing tool or something you would put in a promotional brochure. This is an internal document that defines clear expectations for those who lead within the organization.

In an interview with Dee Ann Turner, a vice president at Chick-fil-A, she said, "Every organization has their own cultural principles that make them unique and sometimes, from organization to organization, the principles sound similar. The real key is how the behaviors of the people of the organization support the culture."[4]

What makes the culture come alive and gives color to it is when the behaviors of the team members embody the desired culture. One of Chick-fil-A's core values is "customer first." That could mean a lot of different things, but the company has a behavior that supports that cultural value. In virtually every Chick-fil-A you walk into, you can expect to hear the words, "How may I serve you?" and "It's my pleasure."

Strong-Culture Companies

To help stimulate your thinking about your own ministry organization, I have included a few samples of strong-culture companies as well as some churches I have worked with.

Southwest Airlines
Live the Southwest Way
Warrior Spirit
- Strive to be the best
- Display a sense of urgency
- Never give up

Servant's Heart
- Follow the Golden Rule
- Treat others with respect
- Embrace our Southwest Family

Fun-LUVing Attitude
- Be a passionate team player
- Don't take yourself too seriously
- Celebrate successes[5]

Zappos

- Deliver WOW through service
- Embrace and drive change
- Create fun and a little weirdness
- Be adventurous, creative, and open-minded
- Pursue growth and learning
- Build open and honest relationships with communication
- Build a positive team spirit and family spirit
- Do more with less
- Be passionate and determined
- Be humble[6]

Tony Hsieh, CEO of Zappos, says, "In determining core values I thought about all the employees I wanted to clone because they represented the Zappos culture well, and tried to figure out what values they personified."[7]

Christ Fellowship Church (Palm Beach Gardens, Florida)

This is not Christ Fellowship Church's complete list, but it is a good sampling of their leadership values and behaviors.

- We are stewards and servants first.

  Am I serving others or do I expect to be served?

- We create environments that are full of it . . . faith, family, fun.
  Am I warm, positive, energetic and prayed up?
- We are thermostats, not thermometers.
  Do I make the room better and brighter when I walk into it?
- Excellence increases influence.
  Am I consistently giving my best and inspiring others to do the same?
- We believe ministry is a "get to," not a "got to."
  Have I thanked God for my being a part of His work?

Harris Creek Baptist Church (Waco, Texas)

Harris Creek has identified five core leadership practices. Notice that under the practice of "speak with candor," they have articulated specific behaviors to define what it means to speak with candor. Although I have not listed all of them below, they have a handful of bullet-point statements under each leadership practice that specifically defines what that practice looks like in everyday ministry life at Harris Creek.

• Speak with candor

A leader is someone who is capable of speaking with candor in all situations. To speak with candor means you are able to:

Say the last 10 percent that needs to be said.

Address any elephants in the room head-on.

Season your language with both grace and truth.

Speak your mind, even at the risk of disagreement, without being a jerk.

• Show your work

A leader is someone who can deliver tangible and measurable results in a timely manner.

• Act like an owner

A leader is someone who thinks and acts on behalf of the entire organization, not just their ministry area.

276

• *Create excellent environments*

A leader is someone who pays attention to details and works to create intentional and excellent environments.

• *Display self-awareness*

A leader is someone who is aware of both their strengths and weaknesses.

North Point Community Church (Alpharetta, Georgia)

North Point has identified and named the staff culture they want to build with six simple, straightforward statements and questions.

• *Take it personally*

How am I personally engaged in our mission and vision?

• *Make it better*

What am I doing personally to help us improve organizationally?

• *Collaborate*

Where am I leveraging the talents and skills of staff outside my primary team?

• *Replace ourselves*

Who am I empowering?

• *Stay fit*

How am I taking care of myself spiritually, physically, relationally, financially, and emotionally?

• *Remain openhanded*

How do I manage the tension triggered by new ideas, innovation, and change?

I encourage you to create your own list of leadership values and practices for your ministry organization. It's a great opportunity to proactively define the unique leadership DNA that you desire for your ministry. And once you create the list of values, courageously live them out. Leadership behaviors tell you not only what you will do but also what you won't do and what behaviors are unacceptable.

As Tony Hsieh at Zappos says, "For individuals, character is destiny. For organizations, culture is destiny."[8]

TEAM DISCUSSION QUESTIONS

1. Whether or not it is officially articulated, what one leadership behavior is an expectation in your ministry?

2. What do you like about the leadership behaviors in the examples of Southwest Airlines and Zappos?

3. From the church examples listed in this chapter, what stands out to you? Why?

4. What is one aspirational value/behavior that perhaps isn't real strong right now in your culture but you desire to strengthen?

PART 8

MOVING FORWARD

Building a healthy and high-performing team is certainly more art than science. Every team is unique. There is no cookie-cutter formula for building a great team. It takes skill and diligence and wisdom and tenacity. Hopefully this book has better equipped you to influence your team environment. I want to conclude the book by giving you a template and a tool. The template is a case study in one of the greatest teams of all time; the tool is a concrete step you can take to galvanize your team's commitment to the mission and to each other.

37

Do You Believe in Miracles?

D o you believe in miracles? Yes." Those were the words uttered by Al
Michaels as the clock hit zero and the 1980 US Olympic hockey team
had just pulled off a David and Goliath moment. This ragtag group of
college students had just defeated the legendary Russian team that had
not lost an Olympic hockey game since 1968. Two days later, the US team
would defeat Finland to win the gold medal.

When the Americans went up 4–3 against the Russians with ten minutes
remaining in the contest, all of America held its breath. It seemed like the
longest ten minutes in history. During those final minutes, goalie Jim Craig
made several fabulous saves that kept all viewers on the edge of their seats.

Sports Illustrated selected that epic hockey game as the greatest sports
moment of the twentieth century—and I wholeheartedly concur. But it was
much more than just a great moment in sports. The Olympic games took
place that year against the backdrop of the Iranian hostage crisis and the
Soviet invasion of Afghanistan. "The so-called Miracle on Ice was more
than just an Olympic upset; to many Americans, it was an ideological
victory in the Cold War as meaningful as the Berlin Airlift or the Apollo
moon landing."[1]

The last generation has seen a long list of uniquely talented athletes.
Think Michael Jordan, Usain Bolt, Serena Williams, Tom Brady, Lindsey

Vonn, and Steph Curry. Part of the greatness of the 1980 Olympic hockey team's story is that there wasn't a superstar. It was a group of no-name college students led by Herb Brooks, who wasn't even the first choice to coach the team. Their journey is a great case study in what it looks like to become a healthy and high-performing team.

Sometime after the Olympics, Coach Brooks shared some of his reflections about this team.

> They were really mentally tough and goal-oriented. They came from all different walks of life, many having competed against one another, but they came together and grew to be a real close team. I pushed this team really hard, I mean I really pushed them. But they had the ability to answer the bell. Our style of play was probably different than anything in North America. We adopted more of a hybrid style of play—a bit of the Canadian school and a little bit of the European school. The players took to it like ducks to water, and they really had a lot of fun playing it. We were a fast, creative team that played extremely disciplined without the puck. Throughout the Olympics, they had a great resiliency about them. I mean they came from behind six or seven times to win. They just kept moving and working and digging.[2]

Several of Coach Brooks's phrases are a great tutorial in how to become a great team.

1. "Mentally tough"

To me, that phrase—"mentally tough"—is about self-leadership. It is about showing up every day with a mind-set to deliver your best. It is about not taking the easy way but rather taking the best way, the way that leads to accomplishing the goal. Mental toughness is about "owning your stuff" and not being a victim. It is about realizing that you are not entitled to anything and that serving on this team is a "get to," not a "have to." It means not being a whiner or complainer but being a problem solver.

2. "Goal-oriented"

All great teams are crystal clear about their objective. They know what the "win" is, and they align their efforts and energies to accomplish the goal before them. The pursuit of a gold medal is a clear and tangible goal. For those of us in ministry, defining the "gold medal" is a little trickier. But because it can be less tangible, it is even more important for us to do the hard work of discerning, praying, and clarifying the win for our ministry. This also means we must have the discipline to say no to the opportunities and ideas that don't lead us toward accomplishing our unique calling.

3. "Grew to be a real close team"

Coach Brooks said that even though these hockey players came from all different walks of life, they "came together." They became a true team. They weren't just *on* a team; they *became* a team. Being on a team means you have a role to play and you do your part. You stay in your lane and make the best individual effort possible. But becoming a team means connecting your part to the overall goal. It means authentically caring about the other players on the team and taking the time to enter into relationship with them. Becoming a team means unselfishly doing what is best for the team and helping others on the team succeed.

4. "Pushed this team really hard"

Not surprisingly, the team showed incredible commitment and an impressive work ethic. You don't halfheartedly stroll into greatness. Coach Brooks set up an extremely rigorous training schedule. The team played sixty-one exhibition games prior to entering the Olympics. One night after a poor exhibition performance against Norway, the team started toward the locker room. Coach Brooks said, "Get back on the ice!" For more than an hour, they did grueling line drills, which the team called "Herbies," named after their coach. After trying to get the team to leave, the custodian turned off the lights, and Coach Brooks had them keep skating in the dark. Representing your country and playing for a gold medal is an incredible honor and worthy of your very best. How much more should that be true for us as we represent the King of Kings and serve in a ministry that has an eternal impact? We make lofty statements like that all the time in ministry. But I think we should really take the time to ask ourselves if we truly believe that. Do your actions and passion and work ethic reflect someone who deep down believes that what you do in ministry matters—and matters for eternity?

5. "Creative team"

It is interesting to me that Coach Brooks talked about being a creative team and being a disciplined team in the same sentence. It reminds me of a famous quote attributed to Aristotle, which says, "Through discipline comes freedom."

In their book *Extreme Ownership*, retired Navy SEALs Jocko Willink and Leif Babin write:

> The more strict we were with our standard operating procedures, the more freedom we actually had to operate faster and more efficiently because everyone knew what to do.
>
> When individual members of the team are highly disciplined, they can be trusted, and therefore allowed to operate with very little oversight.[3]

Disciplined teams in which every member has clear roles and priorities can more effectively adapt to a changing environment.

6. "Great resiliency"

One definition of resiliency is the ability to recover quickly from difficulties. Great teams don't give up. When they get knocked down, they pick themselves up, dust themselves off, and get right back to work. They have a strong spirit of endurance and perseverance.

As I have talked about throughout this book, doing ministry is messy. And doing ministry with a team is even more messy. You are in a battle. Spiritual warfare is real. Sometimes you will experience lack of clarity and communication. You will run into seasons of chaos and dysfunction in your ministry organization. People will let you down and breach your trust. These things just come with the territory. To be a great team you must develop a thick skin and a never-give-up attitude.

It's pretty easy to read a book and gain new insight about teams. And it's fairly easy to sit with your team and discuss these insights. The real challenge is taking the risk to start implementing and living these things out. Building a great team is not easy—it never has been. But it is not an overstatement to say that your ministry's kingdom impact hangs in the balance.

I leave you to ponder a famous quote from Herb Brooks: "Risk something or forever sit with your dreams."[4]

TEAM DISCUSSION QUESTIONS

1. Of the six qualities listed from the 1980 US Olympic hockey team, which one does your team do best? Explain.
2. Which one does your team need to work on? Explain.
3. As you think about your journey through this book, what is the single biggest takeaway for you personally?
4. What is the single biggest takeaway for your team?

38

'Til Death Do Us Part:
Establishing a Team Covenant

As we near the end of this journey called *High-Impact Teams*, I challenge you to take a concrete step in your commitment to becoming a healthy and high-performing team. I want you to consider creating a written team covenant. Merriam-Webster defines *covenant* as "a usually formal, solemn, and binding agreement."[1]

I know the word sounds old school, but I like it. Unlike the words *agreement*, *contract*, or *pledge*, *covenant* has a feel of something more sacred. A covenant is not focused on the letter of the law; it is more focused on the heart. It is not about external compliance; it is about internal commitment.

Every person shows up to a team with a backpack full of beliefs, assumptions, experiences, and hurts that shape their hopes and expectations of team. The problem is that those expectations collide with those of other team members.

A team covenant is a chance to clarify expectations and get everyone to agree on what doing team will look like for your specific team.

Typically teams do not articulate an agreed-on set of values and behaviors that define how you will do team. It is possible to have organizational clarity and team confusion. And you can have functional plans but dysfunctional teams. My observation is that the team culture of many ministry organizations is squishy and loaded with land mines. The result is often tension, frustration, and dysfunction.

That's why leaders must take responsibility to bring clarity to the team culture. Marcus Buckingham has insightfully said, "Clarity is the pre-occupation of the effective leader. If you do nothing else as a leader, be clear."[2]

A team covenant is a tool to bring clarity to the guidelines and guardrails for your unique team.

This is different from the staff behaviors I talked about in the last chapter. The handful of staff behaviors apply to everyone across the organization. A team covenant is more of an internal document for your specific team. Just today I read an article about a Jacksonville Jaguars football player who wasn't able to play in their game this week because he had violated their team rules. The team obviously has some guidelines and expectations for how they do team.

In my opinion, a team covenant should be a fairly brief document (probably one page) that contains eight to twelve statements about how the team will function. Some of the statements might be about how the team members relate to one another personally. Some might be about how the members relate and do team organizationally. I suggest spending the time to make the statements as clear and specific as possible.

I also strongly advise making this a collaborative experience. By making the team covenant a true team exercise, you will elevate the team members' sense of ownership for it. Also, it has been my experience that when the team creates the team covenant, everyone helps monitor it in the actions of the team.

As you sit down to dialogue with your team about a team covenant, here are some questions to help prime the pump:

- What kind of team environment do we want to create?
- What do we do now that is working?
- What causes stress and frustration in our team?
- Where do we have colliding expectations?
- What are some changes that would help us be more healthy and high performing?

- What values do we have that we would like to see in our team rule of life?
- How can we help and support one another personally and spiritually?
- How can we have more effective team meetings?
- What are our values concerning communication and resolving conflict?

Finally, as you craft your team covenant, the following areas might help inform your discussion and what you include in it.

1. Personal health
- Busyness and hurry (margin/Sabbath)
- Family priorities
- Managing technology

2. Spiritual life
- Spiritual practices (i.e., prayer, feeding your soul)
- Importance of Scripture
- Personal holiness

3. Relationships
- How you speak to and treat one another
- Culture of respect and "one another"
- Sense of family/community

4. Leadership
- Learning and personal development
- Investing in and developing others
- Submission to authority

5. Teamwork
- Fun
- Resolving conflict with truth and grace
- Communication

Once you have created your team covenant, don't just let it sit in a computer file somewhere. Make it a living, breathing tool you regularly revisit. I suggest that at least quarterly, you pull out your team covenant and honestly assess how you are doing at living out the guidelines you made with one another.

It is the convergence of clarity of expectation and consistency of inspection that makes the team covenant a game-changing tool.

Notes

Chapter 2 Liquid Teams

1. *The Free Dictionary*, s.v. "synergy," accessed February 19, 2018, https://www.thefree dictionary.com/synergy.

2. Sara Ganim and Linh Tran, "How Tap Water Became Toxic in Flint, Michigan," CNN, January 13, 2016, http://www.cnn.com/2016/01/11/health/toxic-tap-water-flint-michigan /index.html.

Chapter 4 Doing Ministry without Losing Your Soul

1. Henri Nouwen, *In the Name of Jesus* (New York: Crossroad, 2000), 10.

2. Jamin Goggin and Kyle Strobel, *The Way of the Dragon or the Way of the Lamb* (Nashville: Thomas Nelson, 2017), xix.

3. Goggin and Strobel, *The Way of the Dragon*, 13.

4. Ruth Haley Barton, *Strengthening the Soul of Your Leadership* (Downers Grove, IL: InterVarsity, 2008), 13.

Chapter 5 The Greatest Gift You Give Your Team

1. Parker Palmer, *Let Your Life Speak: Listening for the Voice of Vocation* (San Francisco: Jossey-Bass, 2000), 82.

2. Peter Scazzero, *Emotionally Healthy Spirituality: It's Impossible to Be Spiritually Mature while Remaining Emotionally Immature* (Franklin, TN: Integrity Publishers, 2006), 12.

3. Peter Scazzero, *The Emotionally Healthy Leader: How Transforming Your Inner Life Will Deeply Transform Your Church, Team, and the World* (Grand Rapids: Zondervan, 2015), 55.

4. François Fénelon, *The Seeking Heart* (Cambridge, OH: Christian Books Publishing House, 1992), 147.

5. Scazzero, *The Emotionally Healthy Leader*, 30.

6. Palmer, *Let Your Life Speak*, 79.

Chapter 6 I Hate the Word *Balance*

1. Noah BenShea, *Jacob the Baker: Gentle Wisdom for a Complicated World* (Albuquerque, NM: Number Nine Media, 2013), 23.
2. Michael Hyatt, "12 Reasons Why Your Brain Craves Vacation," June 27, 2016, personal email.

Chapter 7 Just Stop It

1. Judy Brown, *The Art and Spirit of Leadership* (Bloomington, IN: Trafford Publishing, 2012), 147–48.

Chapter 8 Please Like Me

1. Judith Hougen, *Transformed into Fire: Discovering Your True Identity as God's Beloved* (Grand Rapids: Kregel, 2002), 65.
2. David Benner, *The Gift of Being Yourself: The Sacred Call to Self-Discovery* (Downers Grove, IL: InterVarsity, 2004), 14.
3. E. E. Cummings, "A Poet's Advice to Students," in *A Miscellany* (New York: Agrophile, 1958), 13.
4. Palmer, *Let Your Life Speak*, 9.
5. Lewis B. Smedes, *Shame & Grace: Healing the Shame We Don't Deserve* (New York: HarperCollins, 1993), 6.
6. Henri Nouwen, *The Life of the Beloved: Spiritual Living in a Secular World* (New York: Crossroad, 1992), 106.

Chapter 9 Management Matters

1. Jeff Shore, "These Ten Peter Drucker Quotes May Change Your World," *Entrepreneur*, September 16, 2014, https://www.entrepreneur.com/article/237484.
2. Barry Demp, "Managers Light a Fire under People. Leaders Light a Fire in People," The Quotable Coach, April 15, 2015, http://www.thequotablecoach.com/managers-light-a-fire/.
3. Warren Bennis, *On Becoming a Leader* (New York: Basic Books, 1989), 42.
4. Peter Lauria, "Michael Eisner on Media's Future," Business Insider, September 10, 2010, http://www.businessinsider.com/michael-eisner-2010-9.
5. Samuel C. Certo and S. Trevis Certo, *Modern Management* (Upper Saddle River, NJ: Prentice Hall, 1997), 6.
6. Master Sergeant Emil W. Zacharaia to Lieutenant Paul Giddens, US Army, 1968, quoted in Ron Ernst, *Real Time Coaching* (Carmel, IN: Leadership Horizons, 1999), 23.

Chapter 10 "Squirrel"

1. Henry Cloud, *Boundaries for Leaders: Results, Relationships, and Being Ridiculously in Charge* (New York: HarperBusiness, 2013).
2. Chris McChesney, Sean Covey, and Jim Huling, *The 4 Disciplines of Execution: Achieving Your Wildly Important Goals* (New York: Free Press, 2012), 8.
3. Carmine Gallo, "Steve Jobs: Get Rid of the Crappy Stuff," *Forbes*, May 16, 2011, https://www.forbes.com/sites/carminegallo/2011/05/16/steve-jobs-get-rid-of-the-crappy-stuff/#5180d0a71452.

4. John C. Maxwell, *Developing the Leader within You* (Nashville: Thomas Nelson, 2000), 28.

5. "Tony Blair," Wikiquote, last modified August 31, 2017, 5:54, https://en.wikiquote .org/wiki/Tony_Blair.

Chapter 11 What Does Success Look Like?

1. McChesney, Covey, and Huling, *The 4 Disciplines,* 13.

2. Jeff Sutherland, *Scrum* (New York: Crown Publishing Group, 2014), 87.

3. Sutherland, *Scrum*, 4.

4. Og Mandino, quoted by Gary Keller, *The One Thing* (Austin, TX: Rellek, 2012), 17.

5. McChesney, Covey, and Huling, *The 4 Disciplines*, 10.

6. Stephen R. Covey, *First Things First* (New York: Free Press, 2003), 88–90.

7. Greg McKeown, *Essentialism: The Disciplined Pursuit of Less* (New York: Crown Publishing Group, 2014), 132–33.

Chapter 12 The Word Nobody Likes but Everybody Needs

1. Bruce Klatt, Shaun Murphy, and David Irvine, *Accountability: Getting a Grip on Results* (Calgary: Bow River Publishing, 2003), 3.

2. Patrick Lencioni, *The Advantage: Why Organizational Health Trumps Everything Else in Business* (San Francisco: Jossey-Bass, 2012), 59.

3. McChesney, Covey, and Huling, *The 4 Disciplines*, 6.

Chapter 13 The Team Equivalent of an IRS Audit

1. Yuki Noguchi, "Yay, It's Time for My Performance Review! (Said No One Ever)," NPR, September 28, 2016, http://www.npr.org/2016/09/28/495795876/yay-its-time-for-my -performance-review-said-no-one-ever.

2. Noguchi, "Yay, It's Time."

3. Jack Welch, "Jack Welch: 'Rank-and-Yank'? That's Not How It's Done," *Wall Street Journal*, November 14, 2013, https://www.wsj.com/articles/8216rankandyank8217-that82 17s-not-how-it8217s-done-1384473281.

4. Marcus Buckingham and Ashley Goodall, "Reinventing Performance Management," *Harvard Business Review*, April 2015, https://hbr.org/2015/04/reinventing-performance-management.

5. Edward E. Lawler, "Performance Management: The Three Important Features You're Forgetting," *Forbes*, April 15, 2015, https://www.forbes.com/sites/edwardlawler/2015/04/15 /performance-management-yet-another/#7b92c6882d9c.

Chapter 14 How to Raise Your Team's Productivity by 30 Percent

1. Jeffrey Scott Klubeck, "The Expense of Ineffective Meetings," Wolf Management Consultants, http://www.wolfmotivation.com/articles/the-expense-of-ineffective-meetings.

2. Lencioni, *The Advantage*, 146.

Chapter 15 ~~Work~~ Stewardship Ethic

1. Tony Mansford and Scott David, "24 Examples of Kobe Bryant's Insane Work Ethic," Business Insider, November 30, 2015, http://www.businessinsider.com/kobe-bryant-insane -work-ethic-2013-8/#he-works-out-harder-and-earlier-than-even-the-nbas-best-players-1.

2. Mansford and David, "Kobe Bryant's Insane Work Ethic."

3. *Despicable Me*, directed by Pierre Coffin and Chris Renaud (Universal City, CA: Universal Pictures, 2010), DVD.

4. Jocko Willink and Leif Babin, *Extreme Ownership: How US Navy SEALs Lead and Win* (New York: St. Martin's Press, 2015), 100.

Chapter 16 "Nailed It!"

1. Theodore Roosevelt, "Citizenship in a Republic," April 23, 1910, delivered at the Sorbonne in Paris, France, transcript, http://design.caltech.edu/erik/Misc/Citizenship_in _a_Republic.pdf.

2. Larry Bossidy and Ram Charan, *Execution: The Discipline of Getting Things Done* (New York: Crown Business, 2002), 19.

3. Bossidy and Charan, *Execution*, 34.

4. Quoted in John Maxwell, *Today Matters* (New York: Center Street Hachette Book Group, 2004), 67.

5. Quoted in McKeown, *Essentialism*, 163.

6. Keller, *The One Thing*, 192.

7. McKeown, *Essentialism*, 182.

8. McKeown, 183.

9. Sutherland, *Scrum*, 89.

10. McChesney, Covey, and Huling, *The 4 Disciplines*, 80.

11. Bill Hybels, *Leadership Axioms: Powerful Leadership Proverbs* (Grand Rapids: Zondervan, 2012), 58–61.

Chapter 17 Just Do It

1. F. M. Alexander, quoted in Keller, *The One Thing*, 119.

2. Kevin Kruse, *15 Things Successful People Know About Time Management: The Productivity Habits of 7 Billionaires, 13 Olympic Athletes, 29 Straight-A Students, and 239 Entrepreneurs* (self-pub., Amazon Digital Services, 2015), loc. 322 of 5258, Kindle.

3. Travis Bradberry, "14 Things Ridiculously Successful People Do Every Day," *Inc.*, May 11, 2017, https://www.inc.com/travis-bradberry/14-things-ridiculously-successful-people-do -every-day.html?cid=ps002ampr.

4. Kruse, *15 Things*, loc. 630 of 5258, Kindle.

5. James Loehr and Tony Schwartz, *The Power of Full Engagement: Managing Energy, Not Time, Is the Key to High Performance and Personal Reward* (New York: Free Press, 2003).

6. Bradberry, "14 Things."

7. Bradberry.

8. Richard Branson, "My One Tip for 2017? Write It Down!" Virgin, January 1, 2017, https://www.virgin.com/richard-branson/my-one-tip-2017-write-it-down.

9. Kruse, *15 Things*, loc. 1247 of 5258, Kindle.

Chapter 18 Techno-Danger

1. Sherry Turkle, *Reclaiming Conversation* (New York: Penguin Books, 2015), 13.

2. Turkle, *Reclaiming Conversation*, 21.

3. Kruse, *15 Things*, loc. 1352 of 5258, Kindle.

Chapter 19 People First

1. Martin Luther King Jr., "Where Do We Go from Here?" August 16, 1967, Eleventh Annual SCLC Convention, Atlanta, Georgia, transcript, https://kinginstitute.stanford.edu /king-papers/documents/where-do-we-go-here-delivered-11th-annual-sclc-convention.

Chapter 20 The Slow Dance of Building Trust

1. Patrick Lencioni, *The Five Dysfunctions of a Team: A Leadership Fable* (San Francisco: Jossey-Bass, 2002), 195.
2. Brown, *Art and Spirit*, 282–83.
3. Patrick Lencioni, *Silos, Politics, and Turf Wars* (San Francisco: Jossey-Bass, 2006), 175.
4. Stephen M. R. Covey and Greg Link, *Smart Trust: Creating Prosperity, Energy, and Joy in a Low-Trust World* (New York: Free Press, 2012), 47.

Chapter 21 Crafting a Culture of "One Another"

1. Bill Hybels, *Axiom: Powerful Leadership Proverbs* (Grand Rapids: Zondervan, 2008), 96.

Chapter 22 "One Another" Best Practices

1. Alan Fadling, *The Unhurried Leader* (Downers Grove, IL: InterVarsity, 2013), 12.

Chapter 23 The Big Brother Syndrome

1. John Townsend, *The Entitlement Cure: Finding Success in Doing Hard Things the Right Way* (Grand Rapids: Zondervan, 2015), 19.
2. Quoted in Scazzero, *Emotionally Healthy Spirituality*, 128.
3. Brad Lomenick, *H3 Leadership: Be Humble. Stay Hungry. Always Hustle.* (Nashville: Thomas Nelson, 2015), 27.

Chapter 24 Getting Comfortable with Uncomfortable Conversations

1. Lencioni, *Five Dysfunctions of a Team*, 188.
2. Kerry Patterson et al., Joseph Grenny, Ron McMillan, and Al Switzler, *Crucial Conversations* (New York: McGraw-Hill, 2012), 9–10.
3. Lencioni, *The Advantage*, 44.
4. Patterson et al., *Crucial Conversations*, 25.
5. A. J. Jacobs, *Guinea Pig Diaries: My Life as an Experiment* (New York: Simon and Schuster, 2009), 56.
6. Susan Scott, *Fierce Conversations: Achieving Success at Church and in Life One Conversation at a Time* (New York: Berkley Books, 2004), xiii–xiv.
7. Scott, *Fierce Conversations*, 166.

Chapter 25 How to Have an Uncomfortable Conversation

1. Howard Berkes, "30 Years after Explosion, Challenger Engineer Still Blames Himself," NPR, January 28, 2016, http://www.npr.org/sections/thetwo-way/2016/01/28/464744781/30 -years-after-disaster-challenger-engineer-still-blames-himself.
2. Bill Zipp, "Beware of This Conversation Killer and Know What to Do about It," BillZippon Business.com, accessed January 18, 2018, http://billzipponbusiness.com/conversation-killer/.

3. Scott, *Fierce Conversations*, 144.
4. Adapted from Scott, 148–53.
5. Scott, 227.

Chapter 26 Inviting an Uncomfortable Conversation

1. Dietrich Bonhoeffer, *Life Together: The Classic Exploration of Christian Community* (New York: Harper & Row, 1954), 105.
2. C. S. Lewis, *Surprised by Joy: The Shape of My Early Life* (San Francisco: HarperOne, 2017), 276.
3. Scazzero, *The Emotionally Healthy Leader*, 64.

Chapter 27 Handling a Hurricane

1. Holland Davis, "Great Response to Dealing with Moral Failure," HD Life In, accessed January 18, 2018, http://www.hollanddavis.com/?p=168.

Chapter 28 Transition Isn't a Four-Letter Word

1. Henry Cloud, *Necessary Endings: The Employees, Businesses, and Relationships That All of Us Have to Give Up in Order to Move Forward* (New York: HarperCollins, 2010), 20.
2. Cloud, *Necessary Endings*, 38.
3. Michael Abrashoff, *It's Your Ship* (New York: Warner Books, 2002), 18.

Chapter 29 How to Transition Honestly and Honorably

1. *Oxford Living Dictionaries*, s.v. "transition," accessed January 23, 2018, https://en.oxforddictionaries.com/definition/transition.
2. Ruth Haley Barton, *Pursuing God's Will Together: A Discernment Practice for Leadership Groups* (Downers Grove, IL: InterVarsity Press, 2012), 63.

Chapter 30 Defining Organizational DNA

1. Megan Friedman, "Merriam-Webster Picks 'Culture' as Its Word of the Year," *Harper's Bazaar*, December 15, 2014, http://www.harpersbazaar.com/culture/art-books-music/news/a4372/merriam-webster-word-of-the-year-culture/.
2. Sam Chand, *Cracking Your Church's Culture Code: Seven Keys to Unleashing Vision and Inspiration* (San Francisco: Jossey-Bass, 2011), 2.
3. Josh Bersin, "Culture: Why It's the Hottest Topic in Business Today," *Forbes*, May 13, 2015, https://www.forbes.com/sites/joshbersin/2015/03/13/culture-why-its-the-hottest-topic-in-business-today/2/#4ecff8445a96.
4. Kai Ryssdal, "Zappos CEO Tony Hsieh: Full Interview Transcript," Marketplace, August 19, 2010, https://www.marketplace.org/2010/08/19/business/corner-office/zappos-ceo-tony-hsieh-full-interview-transcript.
5. Stephen Blandino, "Dave Ramsey's Organizational Culture," StephenBlandino.com, May 24, 2009, http://stephenblandino.com/2009/05/dave-ramseys-organizational-culture.html.
6. Chand, *Cracking Your Church's Culture Code*, 12.
7. McChesney, Covey, and Huling, *The 4 Disciplines*, 105.
8. Bill Peel, "Southwest Airlines' Legendary Corporate Culture: An Interview with Dave Ridley, " Center for Faith and Work at LeTourneau University, accessed January 23, 2018,

http://www.centerforfaithandwork.com/article/southwest-airlines-legendary-corporate-cul
ture-interview-dave-ridley.

Chapter 31 Doing vs. Developing

1. Stephen Blandino, "Developing Leaders: When Leaders Are at Their Best," Stephen Blandino.com, December 15, 2010, http://stephenblandino.com/2010/12/when-leaders-are -at-their-best.html.

2. Subba Rao Chaganti, "12 Leadership Lessons from John Wooden," *BuildingPharma Brands* (blog), February 22, 2013, https://buildingpharmabrands.com/2013/02/22/12-leadership -lessons-from-john-wooden/.

3. McChesney, Covey, and Huling, *The 4 Disciplines*, 74.

4. Wendy Axelrod and Jeanine Coyle, "Deliver Results and Develop People at the Same Time," American Management Association, accessed January 23, 2018, http://www.amanet .org/training/articles/deliver-results-and-develop-people-at-the-same-time.aspx.

Chapter 32 Shock and Awe

1. Daniel Henderson, *Transforming Prayer* (Bloomington, MN: Bethany House Publish- ers, 2011), 27.

2. Nancy Spiegelberg, "Cup or Bucket," Bible.org, accessed February 20, 2018, https:// bible.org/illustration/john-737.

Chapter 33 Growing Christians, Not Just Leaders

1. John Ortberg, *The Life You've Always Wanted* (Grand Rapids: Zondervan, 1997), 47.

2. Peter Scazzero, *Emotionally Healthy Spirituality Day by Day: A 40-Day Journey with the Daily Office* (Grand Rapids: Zondervan, 2014), 10–12.

Chapter 34 Becoming a CCO

1. Dharmesh Shah, "How to Work Out How Good Your Culture Really Is," Culture Incorporated, accessed January 25, 2018, https://www.cultureincorporated.com.au/how -good-is-your-culture-how-to-work-it-out/.

2. Bryan Walker and Sarah A. Soule, "Changing Company Culture Requires a Movement, Not a Mandate," *Harvard Business Review*, June 20, 2017, https://hbr.org/2017/06/changing -company-culture-requires-a-movement-not-a-mandate.

3. Tony Hsieh, *Delivering Happiness: A Path to Profits, Passion, and Purpose* (New York: Business Plus, 2010), 184.

Chapter 35 Culture Tensions

1. "Leadership Summit 2010: Andy Stanley—The Upside of Tension," *Vialogue* (blog), August 5, 2010, https://vialogue.wordpress.com/2010/08/05/leadership-summit-2010-andy -stanley-the-upside-of-tension/.

2. Rick Warren, *The Purpose-Driven Church* (Grand Rapids: Zondervan, 1995), 14.

Chapter 36 It's All about Behavior

1. "Netflix Culture," Netflix, accessed January 25, 2018, https://jobs.netflix.com/culture /#introduction.

2. "Netflix Culture."

3. Will Mancini, *Church Unique: How Missional Leaders Cast Vision, Capture Culture, and Create Movement* (San Francisco: Jossey-Bass, 2008), 54.

4. Henna Inam, "Why Culture Eats Strategy for Lunch at Chick-fil-A," *Forbes*, January 26, 2016, https://www.forbes.com/sites/hennainam/2016/01/26/why-culture-eats-strategy -for-lunch-at-chick-fil-a/#374adad86d85.

5. "Culture," Southwest, accessed February 20, 2018, https://www.southwest.com/html /about-southwest/careers/culture.html.

6. Hsieh, *Delivering Happiness,* 154.

7. Hsieh, 155.

8. Hsieh, 184.

Chapter 37 Do You Believe in Miracles?

1. "1980 US Hockey Team Makes Miracle on Ice," History, accessed January 25, 2018, http://www.history.com/this-day-in-history/u-s-hockey-team-makes-miracle-on-ice.

2. "The 1980 US Olympic Team," US Hockey Hall of Fame, accessed January 25, 2018, http://www.ushockeyhalloffame.com/page/show/831562-the-1980-u-s-olympic-team.

3. Richard Feloni, "Former Navy SEAL Commander Explains the Philosophy That Made His Unit the Most Decorated of the Iraq War," Business Insider, November 10, 2015, http://www .businessinsider.com/retired-navy-seal-explains-why-discipline-is-freedom-2015-11.

4. Charlie Adams, "What We Can Learn from the Miracle 1980 US Olympic Hockey Team," July 15, 2014, HottyToddy.com, http://hottytoddy.com/2014/07/15/what-we-can -learn-from-the-miracle-1980-u-s-olympic-hockey-team/.

Chapter 38 'Til Death Do Us Part: Establishing a Team Covenant

1. *Merriam-Webster*, s.v. "covenant," accessed January 25, 2018, https://www.merriam -webster.com/dictionary/covenant.

2. Marcus Buckingham, *The One Thing You Must Know* (New York: Simon and Schuster, 2005), 146.

Lance Witt is the founder of Replenish Ministries, the author of *Replenish* the book, and is often referred to as a pastor's pastor. Before launching Replenish, Lance served twenty years as a senior pastor and six years as an executive/teaching pastor at Saddleback Church. Lance and his wife, Connie, have two grown children and four granddaughters.

Get connected with

LANCE WITT

at Replenish.net

Who is talking to you...about YOU?

If you and your team could use some help developing healthy lives and a healthy leadership culture, Replenish would be honored to partner with you.

We can provide . . .

- **Personal life coaching**
- **Life planning**
- **Speaking at your event**
- **Team development**
- **Organizational consulting**

If you would like to explore how Replenish might help you and your team, contact us at **info@replenish.net.**

Connect with

Sign up for announcements about new and upcoming titles at

www.bakerbooks.com/signup

 ReadBakerBooks

 ReadBakerBooks